BERLITZ®

IRELAND

1990/1991 Edition

By the staff of Berlitz Guides

10th Printing
1990/1991 Edition

Updated or revised 1989, 1985, 1984, 1982

How to use our guide

- All the practical information, hints and tips that you will need before and during the trip start on page 102.
- For general background, see the sections Ireland and the Irish, p. 6, and A Brief History, p. 14.
- All the sights to see are listed between pages 26 and 87. Our own choice of sights most highly recommended is pinpointed by the Berlitz traveller symbol.
- Entertainment, nightlife and other leisure activities are described between pages 88 and 96, while information on restaurants and cuisine is to be found on pages 96 to 101.
- Finally, there is an index at the back of the book, pp. 126–128.

Found an error or an omission in this Berlitz Guide? Or a change or new feature we should know about? Our editor would be happy to hear from you, and a postcard would do. Be sure to include your name and address, since in appreciation for a useful suggestion, we'd like to send you a free travel guide.

Although we make every effort to ensure the accuracy of all the information in this book, changes occur incessantly. We cannot therefore take responsibility for facts, prices, addresses and circumstances in general that are constantly subject to alteration.

Text: Ken Bernstein
Photography: Eric Jaquier
Layout: Doris Haldemann
We are grateful to Mary Boudren of the Irish Tourist Board and to the Northern Ireland Tourist Board for their substantial help in the preparation of this guide.

Maps based on the Ordnance Survey by permission of the Government of the Republic of Ireland (PERMIT No. 3464).
Cartography: 🌐 Falk-Verlag, Hamburg

Contents

Photo, pp. 2–3: Brandon Bay (Dingle Peninsula).

Ireland
and the Irish

The grass grows greener in Ireland—it's not called the "emerald isle" for nothing. But these spinach-hued pastures alternate with plains of grain, bleak rocky hills, noble mountains and soggy bogs. The fast-changing sky of this unspoiled Atlantic island adds to the drama of the encounter between land and water; you're never more than 70 miles from the sea, and usually within sight of one of the 800 lakes and rivers. The 3,000-mile coastline rises from white sand coves to some of Europe's most dramatic cliffs. Ireland's size—slightly smaller than the state of Maine—doesn't lead to any delusions of grandeur, but there's plenty of room to breathe and air worth breathing on this, the world's 20th largest island.

Scattered amidst all the natural beauties are impressive stone relics of thousands of years of human history. And in the foreground, enhancing all the other attractions, stand the handsome, hospitable people of Ireland. They call foreign travellers "visitors", not "tourists", and extend a genuine, generous "hundred thousand welcomes".

About two-thirds of the island's nearly 5 million inhabitants live in the 26 counties comprising the Republic of

Split personality: Gaelic, English signs over twin doors and windows.

Ireland. The six north-eastern counties, Northern Ireland, remained part of the United Kingdom when the island was partitioned after World War I in an attempt to solve the "Irish problem". The population of the Republic is overwhelmingly Catholic, while in the North the majority is Protestant with strong loyalties to Britain. Years of "troubles" in Ulster have scarred some northern towns but not the countryside. Things in the Republic are approximately as relaxed as ever; the policemen strolling the streets are unarmed and the most serious danger to life and limb comes

from zigzagging, or at best unconventional, Irish drivers.

Aside from the erratic local motorists and ever-stickier traffic in big towns, driving in rural Ireland can still be an old-fashioned pleasure. The open road contributes to the over-all feeling of well-being—not apathy or tropical torpor, but the ability to put life's little problems into perspective.

Those otherwise insatiable colonialists, the Romans, never conquered Ireland, nor attempted to, thus isolating Hibernia (as they named it) from the rest of western European civilization. But invaders and immigrants from other lands arrived to temper the early Celtic culture. When King Brian Boru turned on the Vikings in 1014, his brief victory for the islanders was only the beginning of the nine-century-long suffering and struggle for independence.

The Anglo-Norman conquest of Ireland in 1169 pointed the way to the supremacy of the English language over the bold and colourful Gaelic of the natives. In modern times barely one in a hundred people in Ireland speaks Irish more fluently than English. But the revival of Gaelic, an Indo-European language, has become state policy; it's taught in the schools and printed along with English on official signs and documents. Though everyday use of Gaelic is practically limited to the Gaeltacht—pockets of cultural survival mostly in the west of the island—its syntax, vocabulary and intonation have moulded the distinctive lilting form of English spoken by the Irish. Eloquence in English is not confined to the great Irish authors and playwrights; almost everybody in the country seems to be a witty, articulate conversationalist.

Though a species of palm tree thrives in many an Irish garden, you'd hardly mistake Ireland for a tropical paradise. Nonetheless, the proximity of the Gulf Stream keeps the winters mild. Snow is rare. Rain is not. Significant rainfall is recorded about three out of every four days near the west coast and every second day in the east. Precipitation comes in many degrees—torrential or refreshing or so nebulous it leaves the pavement unmarked. But the sun is never far behind, and the slightest shower is a fine excuse for an Irish rainbow.

Even in metropolis of Dublin, bikes remain popular mode of transport.

The best way to see and know the country is by car. The most inviting beach or historic site may be the one at the end of a spur-of-the-moment detour. Coach tours cover all the highlights with the customary stops for shopping, eating and drinking, and the driver-guides, being Irish, tend to be convivial.

If sightseeing by car or coach is too fast for your taste, you can change the pace and point of view by settling down aboard a horse-drawn gypsy caravan, or spend a week aboard a hired cabin cruiser on a gentle river odyssey. If you've never captained a boat, they'll teach you how. And those tired of conventional hotels can seek out ancient castles refurbished as hotels, or stay in farm homes or thatched cottages.

Sightseers who prefer cities won't be disappointed in Dublin, a stately capital of broad avenues, green parks and harmonious terraces. Dublin can

Irish history in stone: stacked as fences or carved to glory of God.

offer more in the way of museums, galleries and other cultural attractions than many cities its size. The River Liffey cuts through the heart of Dublin to the Irish Sea. Indeed, all the island's important towns take their character from rivers or the sea or both. Belfast, the metropolis of the north, is Ireland's biggest port. Cork, the Republic's second city, was founded by the Vikings on an island of the River Lee. In the west, the River Shannon ex-

plains and beautifies the city of Limerick.

But, by and large, the truly marvellous sights of Ireland are found outside the big towns. The concept of towns is not much more than a thousand years old here. Before that, Ireland was completely rural. The most evocative old buildings were parts of isolated monastic **11** settlements. In many cases, the rural setting plays an intrinsic role in the special quality of the monument.

Natural wonders are as awesome as the Cliffs of Moher or as tranquillizing as the lakes of Killarney, as mystical as the "holy mountain" of Croagh Patrick or as delightful as the horse-breeding prairie of the Curragh. On the way from one place to another, you can savour the more modest but no less memorable pleasures of Ireland: the sight of sheep nibbling the heather on a steep hillside, sails seizing the wind in an enchanted *lough* (lake), freckled farm children waving hello.

In spite of the uncertainties of the weather, the great outdoors is where everything's happening in Ireland. Between the rivers, the lakes and the ocean, there's something exciting for every kind of fisherman. Sailing and boating for their own sake share top billing. While the sea never gets warmer than what might optimistically be called refreshing, splashing about and sunbathing are practised at hundreds of beaches.

Horses figure prominently among the landlocked sports. Ireland has plenty of stables to choose from if you're think-

ing of a riding holiday. Those who admire horses from afar—and Irish horses are admired around the world—can go to the races all year round. The green Irish terrain is also ideal for golf; there are more than a hundred 18-hole courses. And try to catch the national game, hurling, called the fastest field-game in the world.

Shopping is rewarding in Ireland, where the unique handicrafts sell themselves; if the salesmanship were any more relaxed, the shops might just as well shut down. Friendly service also features in the pleasure of eating and drinking in Ireland. The cooks employ some of the world's best meat and fish, so they tend not to fret about fancy recipes. The local whiskey and stout deserve their far-flung fame.

With a glass of something in hand, you can listen to Irish ballads in a wood-panelled pub. Or succumb to the din of a disco den. Concerts, serious and pop, go on all year long, and in the land of Sheridan and Shaw, Beckett and Behan, the curtain never falls on the theatrical tradition.

Nobody can guarantee you a suntan in Ireland, but the beauty of the island and the warmth of the people will burn a place in your heart.

A Brief History

Like all the great, timeless sagas, the story of Ireland is propelled on waves of adventure, challenge and tragedy. To the Irish of today, ancient legends seem as close as yesterday, historic crises as topical as this morning's headlines.

Relics from the Stone Age lead to the general conclusion that Ireland has been inhabited for about 8,000 years. The first settlers may have travelled on foot from Scandinavia to Scotland—England was still linked at that time to northern Europe by land—then across what was a narrow sea gap to Ireland.

During the later phase of the Stone Age, the inhabitants settled down as farmers. Tombs and temples from that period can be found in many parts of the country, usually in the

Eloquent whorls engraved on neolithic tomb and in ancient jewellery.

middle of somebody's pasture. Some of the monuments are as simple as stone tripods; others, as sophisticated as the neolithic passage-graves, built on astronomical alignment and containing mysterious engravings in spiral and zigzag patterns.

New settlers and new contacts with Europe brought Bronze Age weapons and skills. But Ireland lagged behind the continent in the next big technological revolution, the Iron Age. The new technology finally reached the island in the last years of the pre-Christian era, brought by tribes who originated in central Europe. They were fighters worthy of legends, and the language they spoke was Celtic.

The Roman legions which rolled across all of western Europe stopped short at the Irish Sea. This helps to explain why the Irish are so different: they developed their own way of life during the formative centuries of the Roman Empire. Though Irish society was hopelessly decentralized—the sparse population was dispersed across the land, under the sway of scores of bickering mini-kingdoms—a single culture developed. The druids and poets told the legends in a common language, recognizable as the Irish version of Gaelic.

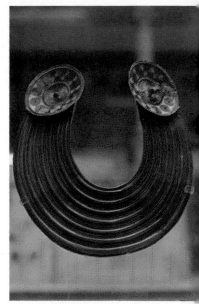

St. Patrick's Day

From time to time, the Celts staged raids on Roman Britain for booty and slaves. In one 5th-century foray the Irish commandos rounded up a substantial number of captives to ease a manpower shortage. One of the involuntary immigrants, a 16-year-old lad, was to become the national saint.

After several years as a shepherd, he escaped to Gaul, heard the call of his life's mission, became a monk and 15 returned to Ireland to convert the heathen to Christianity. St. Patrick's crusade was an incomparable triumph. Ireland is the only western European country in which the pagan surrender was achieved without creating a single Christian martyr.

One of St. Patrick's innovations was the system of monasteries around which all church activities centred. This was well suited to life in Ireland, a rural and skimpily populated island with diverse power blocs. While the rest of Europe crawled through the Dark Ages, the flame of Western culture was kept alight in Irish monasteries. The monks of the "island of saints and scholars" copied the manuscripts of civilization; some of their books were beautiful enough to qualify as major works of art. The early Irish church leaders also founded a missionary tradition which endures to this day.

The first great Irishman to propagate the faith beyond the sea was Colmcille, a poet and scholar of the 6th century who founded the Iona monastery off the coast of Scotland and converted the Picts to Christianity. Colmcille, who became St. Columba, was succeeded by St. Columbanus, whose missionary odyssey covered France, Switzerland, Austria and Italy. At the same time, bright minds from many regions of Europe were converging on Ireland to participate in the flourishing religious and intellectual life.

The Vikings
At the turn of the 9th century, the secure development of Irish society was imperilled by intruders from the north. Well-armed warriors from Scandinavia arrived aboard sleek sailboats in search of booty. Irish monasteries, which contained relics and ornaments of gold and jewels, were easy targets for the Vikings. Their shallow-draught warships attacked virtually at will all around the Irish coast and up rivers as well.

The danger and uncertainty inspired the design of the multi-storey "round tower", Ireland's most original structure of the era. Dozens of these combination watch-towers, belfries, storehouses and escape-hatches are still standing. In most cases the entrance was built high above ground level; the ladder could be hauled up at first sight of a Norse sail.

Viking raids prompted construction of distinctive Irish round towers.

Eventually the traffic became more constructive. The Vikings added commerce to their priorities and established trading colonies on the Irish shore. In fact, they founded the first towns on the hitherto rural island—Dublin, Waterford and Limerick.

The Irish learned sailing skills, weaponry and metal-working from the Norse, but the presence of an occupying force always rankled. Finally the natives ousted the Vikings from Limerick and, later, Dublin. The struggle climaxed in 1014 at the Battle of Clontarf when the High King of Ireland, Brian Boru, took on the Norse and their Irish allies. The king himself was killed, but not before he had given the Vikings a decisive defeat, which has been enshrined in Irish legend.

Cherchez la Femme
Behind the next invasion of Ireland lay many complex

motivations, among them old-fashioned human jealousy.

The tale begins in 1152 when the wife of Tiernan O'Rourke, one of the Irish warrior-kings, was carried off by a political rival, Dermot MacMurrough of Leinster. It's alleged the lady was a more-than-willing victim—or even the instigator. Whether it was a case of abduction or seduction, O'Rourke got his queen back a few months later, but he wasn't about to forgive and forget.

O'Rourke and his allies put so much military pressure on King Dermot that in 1166 he fled to England and then France. Dermot shaped an alliance with a powerful Norman nobleman, the Earl of Pembroke. The earl, known as Strongbow, agreed to lead an army that would sweep Dermot back to power. The other half of the bargain: Strongbow would win the hand of Dermot's desirable daughter and the right to succeed him to the Leinster throne. In the event, the Normans—the élite of Europe's fighting men—won the pivotal battle of Waterford (1169). Then, almost before the flames of battle had been extinguished, Strongbow married the princess in Waterford cathedral.

In further engagements, the Norman war machine stunned and defeated the opposing Norse and Irish forces. Things were going so well for Strongbow that his overlord, King Henry of England, arrived on the scene in 1171 to assert his sovereignty.

Gael and Pale

The Anglo-Norman occupation brought profound, long-lasting changes to Ireland. Towns, abbey-churches and castles were built, institutions of feudal government were established. But the country was never completely conquered. Irish identity remained undiluted; resistance and resentment never flickered out.

For the colonial rulers, the challenge of military revolt was less serious than the danger of assimilation. The settlers were adopting the ways of the natives and not the other way round. In an attempt to enforce a form of apartheid, the Statutes of Kilkenny (1366) forbade inter-communal marriages and banned the Gaelic language. But in practice English was spoken only in the Pale, the area around Dublin where the occupation forces were in complete command.

English control of Ireland was not really consolidated until the House of Tudor turned its attention to the island, making it a training ground for empire. Henry VIII was the first English monarch to add the title of "King of Ireland". After his break with Rome, he tried to introduce the Reformation to Ireland as well as England. But the new religion had influence only in the Pale and in the large provincial towns under English control; everywhere else in Ireland the monasteries and the Catholicism they nourished carried on as before. So did the Irish language.

In the middle of the 16th century, the first implementation of the so-called plantation policy pointed the way to the large-scale redistribution of wealth and the suppression of Catholicism. Desirable farm land was confiscated from Catholics and handed over to Protestant settlers.

The Tudor conquest of Ireland ultimately required a good deal of armed force. During the reign of Queen Elizabeth I, two major revolts had to be put down. Throughout, the most unyielding resistance was centred in Ulster. The Ulster chiefs, led by Hugh O'Neill, tried one last ploy— alliance with Elizabeth's bitterest enemy, Spain. In 1601 a Spanish mini-armada sailed into the southern port of Kinsale. The English defeated both the invaders and the Ulstermen who tried to join them. O'Neill and the leading Ulster aristocrats soon abandoned their land for European exile. The "plantation" programme went on in fits and starts. Most of the land of the north was confiscated and "planted" with tens of thousands of Scots and English, who made Ulster forever different. After 1654, Catholics were only permitted to hold land west of the Shannon, much of it scarcely habitable. "To Hell or Connaught" became the sardonic slogan equating the only alternatives available to the dispossessed.

Religious War
Events in England had their most violent repercussions in Ireland in the middle of the 17th century. Oliver Cromwell and his puritan forces reached Dublin soon after Charles I was executed. Cromwell supervised a campaign against those who had supported the deposed king; the towns of Drogheda and Wexford were special targets for destruction. By the time Cromwell left Ireland in May 1650, the backbone of resistance had been broken.

Ireland again became a bat- **19**

tle-ground when the Protestant William of Orange challenged his Catholic father-in-law, James II, over the succession to the British throne. From exile in France, James sailed to Ireland to mobilize his co-religionists. William came over from England for the showdown, the Battle of the Boyne in July 1690.

The Orangemen, aided by troops from several Protestant countries, outnumbered the combined Irish and French forces commanded by James. As momentous battles go, it set no records for scope or tactical innovation. Nor did it end the war; the losers fled to regroup. But William of Orange was clearly the winner of the Battle of the Boyne, and its anniversary is still celebrated with fervour by Protestants in Northern Ireland.

When the war finally ended with the Treaty of Limerick in 1691, the religious rights of the Catholics were guaranteed. But the all-Protestant Irish parliament soon passed a series of "Penal Laws" to keep all positions of power and influence beyond the reach of the Catholic majority.

Revolutionary Ideas

The victory of the colonists in the American Revolution

Working dogs see their flock safely past the gate in stoney Connaught.

touched off daring new thinking in Ireland. Agitation for greater freedom and tolerance was led by Henry Grattan, an aristocratic Protestant who defended the rights of all Irishmen in the House of Commons in London. Some restrictions were eased and Ireland won a limited measure of autonomy.

Further pressure came from another Irish Protestant, Theobald Wolfe Tone, a young lawyer. He campaigned for parliamentary reform and the abolition of the anti-Catholic laws. The British government tried to ban Wolfe Tone's organization, the United Irishmen, but in 1793 Catholics did win the vote and some other concessions for which he fought.

Five years later, with the United Irishmen in a state of armed rebellion, a French squadron coming to their aid off the coast of Donegal was intercepted by a British naval force. Wolfe Tone was captured aboard the flagship of the infiltration fleet; he was wearing the uniform of a French officer. Convicted of treason, he committed suicide

before his sentence could be carried out.

In 1801 the Irish parliament was abolished. It voted itself out of business after approving the Act of Union establishing the United Kingdom of Great Britain and Ireland. Irish politicians would henceforth sit amongst the M.P.'s at Westminster; the Mother of Parliaments would govern Ireland from afar. The idea was that the economic and political destinies of the two islands would become inseparable. But Irish nationalism never faded away.

A leading opponent of the Act of Union was Daniel O'Connell, one of the first Catholics to win admission to the Irish bar. In 1823 he founded the Catholic Association, which became a mass-movement working for emancipation. He won a landslide victory five years later in a by-election for the House of Commons—but as a Catholic he was legally forbidden to take his seat. To head off further conflict, Parliament passed the Emancipation Act (1829), removing the most severe of the remaining discriminatory laws. O'Connell then turned to a campaign to repeal the Act of Union. Though he failed, he is still remembered in Ireland as "The Liberator".

Starvation and Emigration

One of the worst disasters of 19th-century Europe was the great Irish famine. The first hint of trouble came in September 1845, when potato blight was discovered on farms in south-east Ireland. The British government promptly set up an investigation, but the commission's experts incorrectly diagnosed the outbreak. The next crop was a total disaster nationwide; the staple food of the Irish peasant disappeared. Cruel winter weather and an inevitable outbreak of disease added to the horror of starvation.

The survivors stampeded to flee the stricken land aboard creaking old "coffin ships". Pitiful Irish refugees swamped Liverpool, Halifax, Boston and New York. The tragic toll of the famine is estimated to have reduced the population of Ireland by 2 million: half of them died, the rest emigrated. It took another century before the constant decline in the population figures was reversed and the emigration flow staunched.

Emigrants were among the founders of the Irish Republican Brotherhood—the Fenian movement—a broadly based secret organization dedicated to the overthrow of British rule.

An I.R.B. uprising in 1867 was crushed but the survivors reorganized and planned for a successful revolt. They had to wait 49 years for their big chance.

In the last quarter of the 19th century, two very dissimilar Irishmen led a campaign to return the land to the peasants. The first was Michael Davitt, founder of the Land League, a one-armed revolutionary from a working-class background. The other, Charles Stewart Parnell, who became the league's president, was a Member of Parliament of the Protestant upper class. Together they declared the "land war" of 1879–82, in which great masses of the people became involved. The struggle finally brought down the traditional landlord structure.

(In one incident, a County Mayo land agent refused to cooperate with the reformers. The Land League cut him off so effectively from the rest of the world that the name of the man, Charles Boycott, passed into English as the common word for an organized snub.)

Frustration and Revolt

Toward the end of the 19th century a series of frustrations beset the forces working for Irish autonomy or home rule. Parnell, the shining hope of the Irish cause, lost his influence when he was convicted of adultery with the wife of a fellow M.P. And though home rule legislation was pushed through the Commons, it was rejected in the Lords.

But nationalist sentiment was encouraged from many quarters as distinct as the Gaelic Athletic Association (dedicated to propagating the games of hurling and Gaelic football at the expense of cricket) and the Gaelic League (defender of the declining Irish language). In 1905 several nationalist groups were consolidated in a new political movement called Sinn Fein (Irish for "ourselves").

Home rule legislation, which had been a football in parliament for years, looked more than ever like an abstraction when Britain entered World War I. A group of activists decided that the time would never be more apt for an uprising.

In the Easter Rising of 1916, rebels seized the General Post Office in Dublin and symbolically proclaimed a provisional government for the Irish Republic. The plotters never stood a chance. The authorities soon crushed the insurrection, which in any event had lacked general support. But the prompt, pitiless repression **23**

More than just a place to buy a stamp, Dublin's General Post Office is a revered historic monument: it was GHQ for the Easter Rising of 1916.

which sent the rebel leaders to the firing squad shocked the people and prepared the ground for the successful war of independence.

At the next general election the nationalist Sinn Fein, now led by Eamon de Valera, won by a landslide. De Valera, born in New York of an Irish mother and a Spanish father, had been a battalion commander during the Easter Rising.

Two Irelands

The newly elected Sinn Fein parliamentarians declined to fill their posts in the Commons in London but instead set themselves up in Dublin as Dail Eireann, the parliament of Ireland.

More than two years of guerrilla warfare and government reprisals followed. At last the crisis was cooled by the partition of Ireland in December 1921. Six counties of the north, where the great majority of the population was Protestant and fiercely opposed to rule from Dublin, remained part of the United Kingdom. The other 26 counties, with a Catholic majority, became the Irish Free State, a dominion within the British Empire.

Fervent republicans, who rejected partition and partial links with Britain, unleashed a civil war known as "The Troubles" which shook the brand-new state. Among the casualties during nearly a year of fighting was Michael Collins, the handsome commander-in-chief of the provisional government's armed forces and a legendary independence fighter; he was slain in an ambush in August 1922.

The new country called Eire progressively loosened its ties with Britain. The most conclusive demonstration of the split was Ireland's neutrality in World War II. After the war, the new republic was admitted to the United Nations and undertook an international role, providing troops for UN peace-keeping operations.

When Britain and Ireland joined the European Economic Community, hopes were raised that they might be able to work more closely together. But their deadly mutual problem, the Northern Ireland question, has eluded solution. After years of sectarian violence and intransigence, no way out of the crisis has been sighted; even talking together is controversial. The roots of the conflict go too deep into the island's history.

25

Where to Go

You can't see it all. Ireland's area may be modest but it contains too many worthwhile sights to squeeze into a single vacation. For example, it would take three weeks merely to go along on all the different day-trips which CIE, the national transport company, runs from Dublin alone. Clearly, big decisions have to be made. They will depend on how much time you have, whether you prefer history or natural wonders, and how you're travelling.

The best way to cover Ireland is by car. Various fly-drive package deals make it economically interesting, too. Coach tours are an alternative. On your own, you can see a fair proportion of Ireland by public transport. But aside from the main routes, bus schedules tend to be designed for country folk going to market and not for tourists.

Ancient Ireland was divided into four provinces: fertile Leinster (which includes Dublin), scenic Munster in the south-west, the rugged grandeur of westernmost Connaught, and northern Ulster with its striking coastline. This book covers the high-spots roughly in that order, starting in Dublin and proceeding more or less clockwise around Ireland. But obviously there's not enough space to describe all the sights—or even all the counties. Wherever you go, whatever you see, bear in mind: you'll enjoy Ireland more at an Irish pace.

Dublin
Pop. 1,020,000
(Greater Dublin)

The capital of Ireland is a very European city of low-profile buildings, many of them outstanding examples of 18th-century architecture. Birthplace and inspiration of great authors, Dublin is pervaded by contrasting moods which can affect even the transient visitor: noble avenues and intimate side-streets, chic shopping and smokey pubs, distinguished museums and colleges along with sports galore. In this appealing melting pot of old and new, the traditional lace curtains still mask the windows of modern apartment blocks, and a policeman riding a bicycle reports to headquarters by lapel radio.

The name of Dublin comes from the Irish *Dubhlinn*, meaning "dark pool". But you'll also see a much older Gaelic name on buses and signs: *Baile Átha*

DUBLIN CENTRE

Cliath, "the town of the hurdle ford", which explains why Dublin was originally settled centuries ago—as a place to ford the River Liffey near its exit to the sea. The river, a system of tranquil canals and the nearby Irish Sea all contribute to Dublin's special atmosphere. Seagulls frequent the centre of town; so do the ghosts of Vikings, Normans, Viceroys...and Leopold and Molly Bloom, late of Eccles Street.

O'Connell Street to St. Stephen's Green

The main street of Dublin, **O'Connell Street** is worthy of a major capital, a lasting monument to the Wide Street Commissioners of the 18th century. It is 150 feet across and as straight as the morals of Father Theobald Mathew, the widely admired 19th-century priest known as the Apostle of Temperance. You'll find him commemorated in one of the four monuments down the middle of the roadway. There used to be five. As an anti-British gesture in 1966, unidentified citizens removed the im-

posing Nelson Pillar erected in 1808. Many Dubliners admired the panache and technical skill of the demolition crew that blew it up in the middle of the night.

The best-known landmark of O'Connell Street, the **General Post Office,** has a significance far greater than its postal predominance. The GPO (as it is always known) was the command post of the 1916 Easter Rising and badly damaged in the fighting. A

28 *On Upper O'Connell Street, multi-chimneyed houses, double-decker buses and a monument to Parnell.*

plaque on the front of the building, in Irish and English, and a statue in the main hall mark the historic event.

At the south end of the street, facing O'Connell Bridge, is the large and complicated monument to Daniel O'Connell (1775–1847), "The Liberator", after whom the street and bridge are named.

From the three-arched bridge, almost as wide as it is long, you can look up and down the **River Liffey** and along the embankments. To the east, beyond the "skyscraper" headquarters of the Irish trade unions, rises the copper dome of the majestic 18th-century **Custom House.** Like many buildings along the Liffey, it was all but destroyed in the civil war fighting of 1921, but has been fully restored.

Some of the most interesting old buildings in Ireland, including disused churches, are now occupied by banks. But it may come as a surprise that the

momentous white stone building facing College Green on the south side of the Liffey is the headquarters of the **Bank of Ireland** company. It was built in the 18th century for the parliament of Ireland, but when parliament was abolished (by the Act of Union of 1800), the bank moved in. The grand portico has 22 Ionic columns.

Behind the curved railings at the entrance to **Trinity College** are the statues of two famous alumni—the philos-opher Edmund Burke and the playwright Oliver Goldsmith. Founded by Queen Elizabeth I in 1591, Trinity remains a timeless enclave of calm and scholarship in the middle of a bustling city. For centuries it was regarded as an exclusively Protestant institution; as recently as 1956, the Catholic church forbade its youth to attend Trinity "under pain of mortal sin". TCD, as it is generally called, is now integrated.

Dublin for highbrows: street recital, precious stacks at Trinity library.

The campus is mostly a monument to the good taste of the 18th century, and visitors will enjoy roaming the cobbled walks amongst trimmed lawns, fine old trees, statues and graceful stone buildings. But Trinity's greatest treasure may be found in the vaulted Long Room upstairs in the **Old Library.** Here the double-deck-er stacks hold thousands of books published before 1800, and priceless early manuscripts are displayed in glass cases. Long queues of students and tourists reverently wait for a look at the **Book of Kells.** This 340-page parchment wonder, hand-written and illustrated by Irish monks in the 8th or 9th century, contains a Latin version of the New Testament. The beauty of the script, the decoration of initial letters and words, the abstract designs and **31** above all the saintly portraits constitute the most wonderful survival from Ireland's Golden Age. The leaves of vellum on display are turned once a day to protect them from the light and to give visitors a chance to come back for more.

Some of Europe's finest Georgian houses face **Merrion Square,** once the proposed site for a Catholic cathedral, now a public park. The discreet brick houses have those special Dublin doorways, flanked by columns and topped by fanlights, and no two are alike. In a complex of formal buildings on the west side of the square stands Dublin's largest 18th-century mansion, the home of the Duke of Leinster. Today **Leinster House** is the seat of the Irish parliament, consisting of the Senate (*Seanad* in Irish) and the Chamber of Deputies (the *Dail*, pronounced doyle).

At the entrance to the **National Gallery** of Ireland is a statue of George Bernard Shaw, a Dubliner known locally as a benefactor of the institution. The National Gallery displays some 2,000 works of art, but holds 6,000 more in reserve. Irish artists, reasonably enough, receive priority but important Dutch, English, Flemish, French, Italian and Spanish masters are also well represented. Among those on display, in chronological order: Fra Angelico, Rubens, Rembrandt, Canaletto, Gainsborough and Goya. Rounding out a prize collection of medieval religious art is the gallery's most recent acquisition, two glorious **frescoes** of the 11th or 12th century, delicately lifted from the walls of the Chapel of St.-Pierre-de-Campublic, in Beaucaire (near Avignon), France.

The main entrance to the **National Museum,** another important Dublin institution, is reached from Kildare Street. The museum's collection of Irish antiquities contains all manner of surprises, from ancient skeletons and tools to exquisite gold ornaments of the Bronze Age. The most famous exhibits are the 8th-century **Ardagh Chalice,** the delicately-worked **Tara Brooch** from the same era and the **Shrine of St. Patrick's Bell** (12th century). You can also examine ancient Ogham stones with inscriptions in what might seem a childish way of encoding Latin. And if you don't have time to make a tour of churchyards and far-off monasteries, you can admire

Merrion Square's doorways are part of Dublin's Georgian heritage.

replicas of the greatest carved stone crosses from the early centuries of Christian Ireland.

The south-east part of central Dublin is unusually well endowed with breathing space, thanks to a number of pleasant squares and parks. The biggest—possibly the biggest city square in Europe—is **St. Stephen's Green.** In the 18th century it was almost surrounded by elegant town houses, some of which survive; conservationists despair at the dwindling number. Inside the square is a perfectly delightful park with flower gardens and a man-made lake inhabited by waterfowl. The square contains many sculptures and monuments in varied style, including a memorial to the poet and playwright W.B. Yeats by Henry Moore. Nearby is a bust of Yeat's friend, Countess Con-

Springtime in St. Stephen's Green, fertile refuge in middle of Dublin.

stance Markievicz, the legendary defender of St. Stephen's Green during the 1916 insurrection and the first woman elected to the British House of Commons.

Another statue honours the man who paid for landscaping St. Stephen's Green in 1880. He was Lord Ardilaun, son of the founder of the Guinness brewery. Some thirsty sightseers might be inspired to find a nearby pub and raise a toast to the stout-hearted benefactor.

Medieval Dublin

Dublin Castle was begun in the 13th century on a hill overlooking the original Viking settlement on the south bank of the Liffey. It was largely rebuilt in the 18th century, which explains why it no longer looks like a medieval castle. Over the centuries it served as seat of government, prison, courthouse, parliament and occasionally as fortress under siege —most recently in 1916. Many a visiting head of state has been fêted in the lavishly appointed State Apartments, once the residence of the British Viceroy.

Around the corner from the castle, Dublin's City Hall (formerly the Royal Exchange) was built in the late 18th century in classical style. It contains ancient royal charters and the municipal regalia.

Dublin has not one but two noteworthy cathedrals. And though it is the capital of a predominantly Catholic country, both cathedrals belong to the Protestant Church of Ireland. The reason for two cathedrals is easily explained if you have the time to sift through 12th-century political and religious rivalries. In any case, **Christ Church** is the older of the two, dating from 1038. One unusual architectural **35** touch is the covered pedestrian bridge over Winetavern Street, linking the church and its synod house. This was built in Victorian times but doesn't spoil the overall mood. Otherwise, Christ Church has Romanesque, Early English and neo-Gothic elements. The **crypt,** which extends under the whole church like a vast wine-cellar, is a remnant of the 12th century, when the cathedral was expanded by Strongbow (see p. 18), whose remains were buried here. However, the authenticity of the present Strongbow tomb—the statue of a recumbent cross-legged knight in armour in the southern aisle—is discounted.

A short walk south from Christ Church leads to Dublin's newer and larger cathedral, **St. Patrick's,** dedicated to the national saint. It is said that St. Patrick himself baptized 5th-century converts at a well on this site; a stone slab which covered the well is displayed in the north-west corner of the cathedral. This church was consecrated in 1192, but the present structure dates mostly from the 13th and 14th centuries. The cathedral is best known for its association with Jonathan Swift, the crusading satirist, who was appointed dean in 1713 and served until his death in 1745. Many Swiftian relics may be seen in a corner of the north transept, and a simple brass plate in the floor near the entrance marks his grave. Next to it is the tomb of the mysterious Stella, one of the two great loves of his life. Over the doorway to the robing room is his own bitter epitaph, in Latin: "…Savage indignation can no longer gnaw his heart. Go, traveller, and imitate, if you can, this earnest and dedicated defender of liberty."

The talented choirboys of St. Patrick's Cathedral lift up their voices—and the spirits of the listeners—at services every day except Saturday. The Cathedral Choir School was founded in 1432. A joint choir from both cathedrals was first in the world to sing Handel's *Messiah* when the composer was in Dublin in 1742. A 1799 copy may be seen in Marsh's Library, next to St. Patrick's. This was Ireland's first public library, founded in 1701.

The North Bank

The most impressive building on the north bank of the Liffey is the domed home of the **Four Courts** (originally Chancery, Common Pleas, Exchequer and King's Bench). It's the work of James Gandon, the 18th-century English-born architect who also designed Dublin's Custom House. The courthouse was quite seriously damaged by prolonged shelling during the civil war in 1922. After lengthy reconstruction it was restored to its original use, and justice continues to be dispensed in the neo-classic Four Courts. Carrying on the tradition introduced by the British, Irish lawyers in action wear wigs and gowns.

St. Michan's Church, around the corner in Church Street, was founded in 1095 and rebuilt several times since. Among curiosities on view is a so-called Penitent's Pew in which sinners had to confess to the congregation. In the vaults, wood coffins and many a mummy can be seen in a remarkably healthy state of preservation. Some of them have been here for over 200 years, saved from normal deterioration, perhaps, by the dry air or its high methane content. It's all a bit spooky.

The last great official building designed by James Gandon, the **King's Inns,** is the headquarters of the Irish legal profession. It contains an important law library and a magnificent dining hall decorated with the portraits of judges.

On the north side of Parnell Square is Charlemont House, one of Dublin's best 18th-century mansions. Now the **Municipal Gallery of Modern Art,** it includes pieces from the superb collection of Sir Hugh Lane. He was drowned in the *Lusitania* disaster of 1915, provoking a long legal struggle over custody of his paintings. For 20 years pictures shuttled back and forth between Dublin and London. The latest agreement assures the Municipal Gallery three-fourths of the contested legacy, including works by Corot, Courbet, Manet, Monet and Rousseau.

Beyond the Centre

The **Phoenix Park** provides Dubliners with nearly three square miles of beautiful parkland on the western edge of the city. The most conspicuous monument, overshadowing flower gardens, forests and sports fields, is an immense obelisk commemorating the military victories of the Duke of Wellington. He happened to be born in Ireland but later quipped ungraciously that although a man may be born in a stable, that doesn't make him a horse.

Among the buildings discreetly planted in the park is the residence of the president

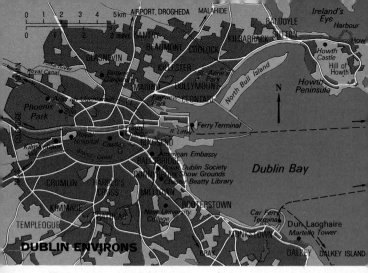

of Ireland (*Aras an Uachtarain*).

On the north-east side of the park, the Dublin **zoo** provides education and diversion. If you can't distinguish an ostrich from an emu, the informative signs will remove all doubts. The zoo is noted for breeding lion cubs in captivity.

In Kilmainham, a half-mile south of the park on the South Circular Road, a stone tower-gate in a style sometimes reviled as "gingerbread gothic" guards the grounds of the **Royal Hospital.** The building within, Dublin's principal 17th-century monument, was a home for army pensioners, now an exhibition centre.

An ugly, forbidding structure, **Kilmainham Jail** has been painstakingly restored as if it were a work of art. But its relevance is historic not aesthetic. The prisoners who lived and died within its walls include many heroes of Irish nationalism. Guided tours are organized every Sunday afternoon. The central cellblock now features exhibitions from Irish revolutionary history.

Jails are unlikely tourist attractions, and so are factories. But many a pilgrim makes his way to the biggest industrial enterprise in Dublin, the **Guinness Brewery** at St. James's Gate. The firm has been on this site since 1759 and its dark, full-bodied stout is known far and wide. Visitors are shown a film about the manufacturing process and invited to sample the finished product so much a part of Irish life. There's also an art gallery on the premises, featuring changing exhibitions of modern art.

In the Ballsbridge district of south-east Dublin are the spacious grounds of the **Royal Dublin Society** (RDS). A green and golden privet hedge surrounds the fields on which one of the world's great horse shows is held every August. The RDS complex is also the site of agricultural and industrial exhibitions as well as conferences and concerts.

This area of parks and large residences contains many foreign embassies, especially in Ailesbury Road. Around the corner in Shrewsbury Road is the **Chester Beatty Library and Gallery of Oriental Art.** The collection is known for its priceless manuscripts and miniatures from the East: jade books from the Chinese imperial court, early Arabic tomes on geography and astronomy and a sampling of Korans. The collector and donor was Sir Alfred Chester Beatty (1875–1968), an American who retired in Ireland.

Dublin Daytrips

The north-eastern extremity of Dublin Bay, the Howth peninsula, makes an appealing start for out-of-town excursions. From its high-point, the 560-foot-high Hill of Howth, you can survey the bay and the open sea. HOWTH HARBOUR, on the north side of the peninsula, is an important commercial fishing port as well as an agreeable haven for pleasure boats. From here you can see and visit IRELAND'S EYE, a craggy islet a mile offshore popular with birds and bird-watchers.

MALAHIDE, a small resort town, is best known for its **castle,** a two-turreted medieval pile with a lived-in look. The spirit of the Talbot family, who resided here for 791 years, still fills the place—not only with the portraits on the walls but even the colour of the paint behind them, "Malahide orange", a tint found nowhere else. Much of the National Portrait Collection, from the National Gallery in Dublin, is also on show here. Sumptuous lawns surround the castle, which was bought by the Dublin County Council after the death of the last Lord Talbot in 1975.

Drogheda, an industrial **39**

town with a population of 24,000, straddles the River Boyne near the site of the fateful battle of 1690 in which James II lost his chance to recover the English crown. This once important medieval city was surrounded by a stone wall with ten gates. You can still drive through the 13th-century **St. Lawrence's Gate,** with its two high towers standing vigilantly as ever. In the centre of town, the neo-Gothic **St. Peter's Church** is dedicated to St. Oliver Plunkett (1628–81), Archbishop of Armagh, who was executed by the British in connection with an alleged Popish Plot. Relics of the local saint are displayed in the church. They include the actual door of his cell at Newgate Prison and, most amazing of all, the embalmed head of the martyr, kept in a gold case in a side altar.

Six miles to the north-west is **Monasterboice** (St. Buithe's Abbey), one of the ancient Irish monastic settlements. Above it all stands the jagged top of what is thought to have been the tallest **round tower** in Ireland, 110 feet high. Along with the remains of two ruined churches you can see three important examples of early Christian **high crosses.** Many of the intricately carved figures

portray New Testament subjects, but others are enigmatic or abstract.

A five-storey medieval gatehouse sternly guards the approach to **Mellifont Abbey,** Ireland's most important early Cistercian monastery. The buildings include the remains of a large church and, nearby, the **Lavabo,** an unusual and graceful octagonal building of which only four sides remain. Like most of Ireland's abandoned monastic institutions,

Mellifont is set amidst the most peaceful, verdant farming country.

Newgrange, a massive Neolithic tomb, looks like a manmade hilltop. It is an astonishing feat of prehistoric engineering, not least because the narrow tunnel leading to the central shrine was positioned to let the sun shine in precisely on the shortest day of the year, December 21. Newgrange, on the north bank of the Boyne, is considered one of Europe's best examples of a passage-grave. The 62-foot-long tunnel is high and wide enough for a modern tourist to go through in a crouch. At the end of it you can stand in the circular vault and look up at the high ceiling and marvel at the 4,000-year-old construction technique. Intriguing carvings, mostly spirals, circles and dia-

Ruins of Trim Castle brood over rustic countryside of Boyne Valley.

mond designs, decorate stones in the inner sanctum and at the entrance. Outside, a dozen large upright stones, about one-third of those originally placed here, form a large protective circle around the mound. Two other large Neolithic tumuli have been found in the area, at KNOWTH and DOWTH, suggesting that this was a very special place in prehistoric times.

Scribes and artists of the monastery at **Kells,** County Meath, are credited with producing the nation's most beautiful book, now on display at Trinity College, Dublin. The town of Kells has grown up around the monastic settlement; a fine Celtic cross stands at the main traffic intersection. Near the cemetery are several other high **stone crosses** and a **round tower,** almost completely intact and almost 100 feet high.

As its name seems to indicate, **Trim** is a well-kept, tidy town. In fact, the terse English name is derived from the Irish *Baile Atha Truim,* meaning the town of the Elder-Tree Ford. The river in question is the Boyne, which adds greatly to the beauty of the place. Trim claims to have Ireland's largest medieval **castle,** a former Norman stronghold. Vast it is, but time has left little more than

the bare bones. To the south, the Dublin Gate, with a pair of drawbridges, contained a prison. On the opposite side of the river, the so-called Yellow Steeple resembles a finger pointing heavenward. It was part of an Augustinian abbey established in the 13th century. The tower was blown up deliberately to keep it out of the hands of Cromwell.

West of Dublin, landlocked County Kildare has some of the greenest pastures in Ireland, or anywhere. It's also a great part of the world for sporting folk. But there is no shortage of historic sites amid the rolling hills.

Maynooth, a pleasant university town with the remains of a 12th-century castle, has gained renown as a training-ground for priests. St. Patrick's College, founded in 1795, is considered one of the world's foremost Catholic seminaries.

On the edge of the village of CELBRIDGE, **Castletown House** stands at the end of a very long avenue of lime trees. This superlatively stately home in the colonnaded Palladian style has been restored and refurnished with 18th-century antiques and paintings. Castletown House was built in 1722 for the speaker of the Irish House of Commons, William

Connolly. A few miles from the house, Speaker Connolly's widow ordered the construction of a monstrous triumphal obelisk. Known today as Connolly's Folly, it was erected with the best of intentions, to provide employment for local workers suffering through the great famine of 1740.

The administrative centre of the county, a town called NAAS (from the Irish *Nas na Ri*, Assembly-Place of the Kings), has an important race-course. So does nearby PUNCHESTOWN. But the capital of Irish horse-racing and breeding is the **Curragh,** a fabulous prairie stretching from DROICHEAD NUA (meaning New Bridge) all the way to Kildare town. Even when you know what to expect, it's a shock to come upon a big, modern grandstand—site of the Irish Sweeps Derby—in the middle of this endless plain.

Many of the winners of the world's richest races were born at the **National Stud** at TULLY. Here thoroughbreds live in what closely resembles a first-class motel. Visitors are al-

Big decisions: in the Curragh, the capital of Irish racing, enthusiasts study the investment possibilities.

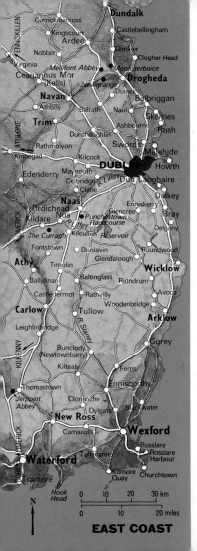

EAST COAST

lowed from Easter to October. The Irish Horse Museum on the premises credits the Celts with inventing the horse-shoe.

As a sort of side-show to the main event, an immaculate **Japanese garden** adjoins the Stud. In the beginning of the 20th century, one Japanese gardener and 40 local men worked for four years to transform an Irish bog into a little world of sheared shrubs, disciplined trees, a lotus pond and even a teahouse and a red wooden bridge.

The town of **Kildare** is also remembered for the double monastery (monks and nuns) founded there by the 5th-century St. Brigid. The buildings were badly damaged by the Vikings and other invaders. But the present 19th-century **cathedral** (Church of Ireland) incorporates 13th-century elements. Nearby you can inspect an ancient **round tower** in very good shape. This one has stairs all the way to the summit.

The ruins of yet another ancient monastery are found at the southern end of County Kildare, in the village of Castledermot. Two beautifully carved high crosses remain, as well as the portal of a church that could be a thousand years old. The design of this lonesome ruin has been neatly repeated in a new church just a few yards behind it.

South of Dublin is Ireland's top yachting centre, **Dun Laoghaire.** The stone piers protecting the harbour are each about a mile long, leaving plenty of space between them for a fleet of pleasure boats and the car ferry terminal. Construction of the artificial harbour was considered a great achievement of 19th-century marine engineering and it's still impressive. Dun Laoghaire, Dublin's largest suburb, is pronounced approximately Dunleary.

About a mile to the south at SANDYCOVE, stands a well-maintained 18th-century **tower.** James Joyce once lived in it, and he used the experience to great effect in the opening of *Ulysses.* The Martello tower (named after a town in Corsica) was part of a network of coastal defences erected to ward off an invasion by Napoleon. It has been turned into a Joyce museum.

Another Martello tower may be seen on DALKEY ISLAND, the largest of a group of islands off the appealing resort town of DALKEY.

Just across the border in County Wicklow, the popular resort of **Bray** has a mile-long sand-and-shingle beach backed by an extensive esplanade. Though the Wicklow coast is mostly sandy and low-lying, the interior of the county is known as the Garden of Ireland.

West of Bray, near the somnolent village of ENNISKERRY, is the most majestic formal park you're ever likely to see. The estate of **Powerscourt** descends in disciplined terraces to a lake with a fountain in the middle. The extensive property takes in acres and acres of varied, spectacular scenery. At the centre of it all is an 18th-century 100-room mansion, unfortunately badly damaged in a 1974 fire. But all was not lost: the trees, shrubs, flowers, statues, gates and fountains are as beautiful as ever. The grounds are open from Easter to October. The Powerscourt Waterfall, several miles south of the house itself, may be visited all year round.

Many Irish cemeteries have an awesome sense of continuity between the present and the very distant past. In the ruins of the ancient monastic city of **Glendalough** there are tombstones hundreds of years old alternating with newly covered graves. The original gateway to the settlement still stands, the only one of its kind left in Ire-

land. Inside, on the right, a cross-inscribed stone may have marked the limit of sanctuary granted to those who took refuge within the monastery. As you enter the site, in a narrow wooded valley, you suddenly see the thousand-year-old **round tower,** almost perfectly preserved. With its graceful tapered shape and conical roof, it might almost be mistaken for a missile on the launching pad. The tower was the place to wait out any sieges; its doorway is 11½ feet above the ground, enough to discourage even the lofty Vikings.

The hermit St. Kevin founded the monastery in the 6th century. Inspired by the breathtaking scenery and its remoteness, he planned it as a small, simple contemplative institution. But as its fame spread, Glendalough of the Seven Churches became an important monastic city. It was wiped out by the Anglo-Norman army in 1398. The **ruins** of the churches and associated buildings are especially evocative because of the wild beauty of the setting.

Beyond the clipped formality of the vast Powerscourt estate rise the untamed hills of eastern Ireland.

South-East Ireland

The meteorological service confirms statistically what everyone has always believed: on the average, over the whole year, the south-east enjoys up to an hour more sunshine a day than other parts of Ireland. The better to see—and enjoy—varied scenery, mountains and pastures, rivers and beaches, and picturesque old towns.

Enniscorthy (the Irish *Inis Coirthe* means Rock Island) is a colourful inland port on the River Slaney, which is navigable from here to Wexford. High above the steep streets of the town, Vinegar Hill is a good vantage point for viewing the countryside. It was the scene of the last battle of the 1798 Rising, during which the British General Lake overwhelmed the Wexford rebels armed with pitchforks and pikes, dashing the struggle for independence. Enniscorthy Castle, in the centre of town, is a Norman keep rebuilt in the 16th century and recently opened as a folk museum.

Wexford, the county seat (15 miles to the south), was one of the first Viking settlements in Ireland. In the 9th century it was called *Waesfjord,* meaning the harbour of the mudflats. At **47**

low tide the original name still seems appropriate.

Reminders of the town's seafaring past are on view in an unusual Maritime Museum, housed aboard a former lightship moored at the main quay. Nearby, at Crescent Quay, stands a statue of an 18th-century County Wexford man, John Barry, who went west to become the first commodore of the United States Navy.

Few ancient monuments survive, but they are well signposted. So are the ones which have disappeared; dozens of informative plaques explaining just about every legend in Wexford add to the interest of strolling the back streets.

In October, the Wexford Opera Festival attracts international performers and fans for the presentation of little-known works. The town is also proud of its year-round cultural activities.

South-east of Wexford, the popular resort of **Rosslare** boasts a 6-mile crescent of dune-backed beach. Beyond is ROSSLARE HARBOUR, where car ferries connect with Fishguard, Le Havre and Cherbourg.

Another nautical note before turning inland. At the tip of the Hook peninsula, the southernmost point in County Wexford,

stands a 700-year-old lighthouse which warns mariners of the rocks and signals the entrance to Waterford Harbour. But that's only half the story. A light has been kept burning at HOOK HEAD for the last 1,500 years.

The Norse established seaports like Dublin and Wexford,

Even if it's not quite bathing-suit weather, the beach draws a crowd.

but it never occurred to them to found permanent settlements inland. It was the Normans who moved 20 miles up the estuary to build the town of NEW ROSS, still an important inland port. In the middle of the 13th century, it was encircled by a defensive wall. Dutch-style houses line the waterfront.

The isolated hamlet of DUNGANSTOWN, near New Ross, was the birthplace of the great-grandfather of John F. Kennedy. A plaque marks **49** the white cottage from which he emigrated to Boston.

The slain American president was greatly admired in Ireland; you can see his picture hanging like an icon on some living-room walls. A group of Irish-Americans and the Irish government combined forces to develop the **John F. Kennedy Park,** above Dunganstown. It's an appealing green memorial containing mighty oak and chestnut trees, shrubs, flowers and trimmed lawns. Visitors can follow signposted walks or have a picnic.

Heading south-west into County Waterford, we cross the historic frontier between Leinster and Munster. Largest in area of Ireland's four provinces, Munster includes cities like Cork and Limerick as well as thinly inhabited farmland and romantic Atlantic shores.

The city of **Waterford** (population 40,000) is a busy port about 18 miles from the open sea. From the far side of the River Suir, its long quay presents a very European appearance. Waterford's foundation can be traced back to the 9th century, but the first charter wasn't granted until 1205, by

Medieval stonework at Cashel; in Waterford (right) tradition lives on.

King John of Magna Carta fame. Many municipal mementos are preserved within **Reginald's Tower,** the city's most venerable building. The walls of this massive circular fortification, 10 feet thick and about 80 feet tall, have survived many a siege since they went up in the year 1003. The tower has served as fortress, arsenal, mint, barracks and prison, and now it contains the Waterford Civic Museum.

An elegant Georgian street, the **Mall,** begins at the Quay. Waterford City Hall, built in the 1780s, has many distinguished features including a couple of little theatres and a Council Chamber illuminated by a splendid chandelier of, logically, Waterford glass. The golden age of Waterford glass ran from 1783 to 1851. After a century's lapse, production was resumed, and the largely traditional processes can be seen on guided tours of the factory, a few miles from Waterford centre on the Cork road. It's best to check with the local tourist office in advance.

Castles and Kings

The inland counties of Tipperary and Kilkenny have beautiful river valleys and imposing ruins from a regal past. Tipperary was once the home of the kings of Munster; Kilkenny entered history as the ancient Kingdom of Ossory.

County Tipperary's principal town is CLONMEL (*Cluain Meala* in Irish, meaning Honey Meadow). A hamlet probably existed here on the peaceful River Suir even before the arrival of the Vikings. The town **51** was walled in the 14th century; parts of the fortifications may still be seen. The turreted West Gate was rebuilt in 1831 on the site of one of the original town gates.

The name of the town of **Cahir** is a mercifully abbreviated version of the Irish for Fortress of the Dun Abounding in Fish. The setting on the River Suir is both fetching and strategic. Upstream from the bridge, a family of swans bob above the weir; downstream a seemingly impregnable castle guards the crucial crossing. Built on the river's lovely islet—a site fortified since the 3rd century—the present **castle** may date from the 15th century, or quite possibly earlier; the records are vague. It's in a fine state of restoration now and well worth a visit. Guided tours point out the many military details—musket slits, portcullis, and a cannonball embedded high in one of the walls.

Don't miss **Cashel** (Co. Tipperary), where glorious historic ruins crown a hilltop surveying a thoroughly enchanting green countryside. On the **Rock of Cashel,** a 200-foot-high outcrop of limestone in the middle of a pasture, the kings of Munster made their headquarters from the 4th to the beginning of the 12th century. When St. Patrick

visited here in 450, he baptized King Aengus and his brothers. The hill was handed over in 1101 to the ecclesiastical authorities, who built a precious Irish-Romanesque church on it.

Cormac's Chapel (consecrated in 1134) is different from all others because it was built by Irish monks interpreting the architectural styles they had studied as missionaries in Europe. It has a steeply pitched stone roof, rows of blank arches and two strangely positioned towers. Remarkable stone-carvings of beasts and abstract designs decorate the doorway and arches. An almost whimsical unconventionality distinguishes the whole project.

The chapel is dwarfed by the **cathedral** which abuts it. This 13th-century structure has unusually thick, well-preserved walls. The roof, however, collapsed in the 18th century. This lets the sunlight stream in, helping to clarify the many architectural details of interest as well as some exquisite medieval stone-carvings.

St. Patrick's cross, inside the entry gate, is one of the oldest crosses in Ireland. It looks it. The sculptures on both sides are severely weatherbeaten. The cross rises from the

"Coronation Stone", reputed to have been a sacrificial altar in pagan times.

With all the incomparable structures on the Rock of Cashel, the almost perfect round tower which looms above them seems somehow anticlimactic.

The marketing town of THURLES has some varied claims to fame. It was here in 1174 that the Irish forces inflicted a demoralising defeat on the Anglo-Norman army commanded by Strongbow. Seven hundred years later Thurles was the birthplace of the Gaelic Athletic Association, now a vast amateur sports organization. The town's most conspicuous landmark, the Catholic Cathedral, is a 19th-century impression of the Romanesque style. The square bell tower, 125 feet high, can be seen for miles around.

Four miles south of Thurles, on the west bank of the Suir, **Holy Cross Abbey** has a 12th-century church still in daily use. The name of the church refers to a particle of the True Cross which was enshrined in this Cistercian abbey for centuries. Though construction of the church was begun in Romanesque style, the rebuilding and expansion programs over the following centuries evolved into Gothic. The solid white walls, enhanced by delicate window-tracery, reach up to a perfectly restored 15th-century stone ceiling. Experts acclaim the sedilia, the triple-arched recess containing seats of honour, carved out of black marble and decorated with ancient coats of arms. Another unusual survival is the night stairs, down which the monks stumbled from their sleeping quarters at 2 a.m. to chant matins. One of the bells in the tower was cast in the early 13th century, making it Ireland's oldest.

Kilkenny is a town with a colourful past and present. Among other surprises you will find, smack in the traffic-clogged centre of the city, an enormous medieval castle with acres of lawns—and a river to boot.

This was the capital of the Kingdom of Ossory, one of several small, feuding realms in pre-Norman Ireland. A parliament which convened here in 1366 passed the notorious but ineffectual Statute of Kilkenny to segregate the native Irish from the Anglo-Normans; intermarriage was equated with high treason. In the 17th century an independent Irish parliament met in Kilkenny for several years. Cromwell be-

53

sieged the town in 1650, suffering heavy losses but finally capturing it.

The Irish word for Kilkenny, *Cill Choinnigh*, means Canice's Church. **St. Canice's Cathedral,** built in the 13th century, is probably located on the site of the original ancient church which gave the town its name.

Cromwell's rampaging troops badly damaged the building, but it has since been restored to an admirable state. There are interesting medieval sculptures and monuments throughout the Protestant church. Alongside is a round tower, part of the ancient church, so tall, slim and austere that it resembles a factory smokestack.

Kilkenny Castle was built in the 13th century to replace the primitive fortress erected by Strongbow. The Butler family,

Taking advantage of a break in the rain, visitors walk through grounds of 13th-century castle in Kilkenny.

one of the great Anglo-Norman dynasties, held the castle until 1935. The state now owns it. Three of the original four corner-towers remain. A brilliantly restored picture gallery occupies the upper floor of the north wing.

The streets of Kilkenny (population 17,000) are full of busy, colourfully painted shops. In High Street, the Tholsel, or town hall, an arcaded building of the 18th century, sports a singular eight-sided clock-tower rather like a misplaced lighthouse.

The Kilkenny Archaeological Society runs a museum in **Rothe House**, a Tudor townhouse dated 1594. The exhibits range from Stone Age tools unearthed locally to medieval relics.

Near Thomastown (Co. Kilkenny) you can visit the partially restored ruins of **Jerpoint Abbey**, an ancient Cistercian monastery. Founded in the middle of the 12th century by the king of Ossory, it had a comparatively brief and troubled history. There were rivalries with neighbouring institutions, government pressures to keep out Irish monks and finally the dissolution of the monasteries in 1540.

Parts of the church retain the early Irish-Romanesque lines, but the square central tower with its typical stepped battlements was added in the 15th century. Much sculptural work in the half-restored **cloister** and in the church itself is almost intact. Bigger-than-life-sized **carvings** of knights and ecclesiastical figures make an inspiring monument not only to those they honoured, but to the talented sculptors who worked at Jerpoint in the Middle Ages.

The South-West

County Cork

Ireland's southernmost, and largest, county mixes undulating green farmland with rocky peninsulas and delectable bays. The people are witty and chatty; after all, this is the home of the blarney.

Cork City (pop. 150,000) enjoys all the facilities—and traffic jams—of an important commercial and industrial centre, but the atmosphere is entirely its own. Perhaps this is because of the River Lee of which the poet Edmund Spenser wrote:

The spreading Lee, that like an island fayre
Encloseth Cork with his divided flood…

55

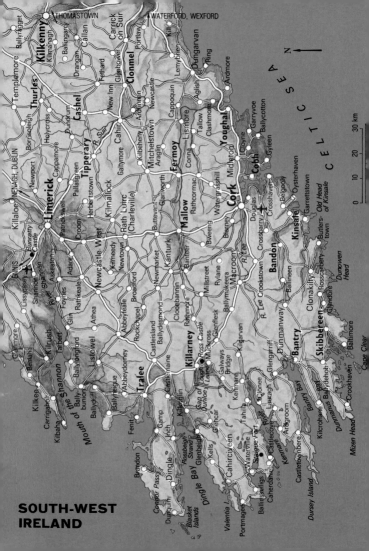

SOUTH-WEST
IRELAND

The dark green waterway that attracts seagulls, swans and giant freighters to the centre of town accounts for much of the mood. So do the steep hills which bracket the urban valleys and its historic landmarks, of which Corkonians are proud and sentimental.

The name of the city has nothing to do with trees or bottle stoppers. Cork is an anglicization of *Corcaigh*, unpromisingly translated Marshy Place. Which is how the area looked in the 6th century when St. Finbarr arrived to found a church and school. In 820 the Vikings raided marshy Cork, destroying the institutions and houses. But they liked the lie of the land and returned to build their own town on the same site. The pattern of destruction and rebuilding was repeated in the 17th century and yet again in the "troubles" of 1919–21.

Seeing any city afoot permits a closer look at the monuments and people. In Cork, you can follow a signposted walking tour, marked by green-and-white "Tourist Trail" symbols, that takes in the most important sights. But you have to begin at the tourist office in the stately Grand Parade, where they sell the booklet explaining the numbered trail. Some highlights:

Red Abbey. The only vestige of the medieval monasteries of Cork. The Duke of Marlborough is said to have watched the siege of the city (1690) from its tower: his artillery fired at the town walls from the garden below.

St. Patrick Street. The wide main street of Cork is curved because it covers a river channel. First-class window-shopping and people-watching; the throngs appear on Saturday afternoons.

St. Finbarre's Cathedral (Church of Ireland). The latest version, 19th century, follows the lofty French-Gothic style, with arches upon arches; some staid modern statues.

Shandon Church. The pepper-pot belfry has long been a favourite city landmark. Visitors can climb up through the clockwork intricacies and play a tune on the bells.

And all over town, the **quaysides** are fascinating for views of the river, bridges and boats, the city skyline and the hills beyond.

Cork is a good centre for excursions. Five miles to the north, **Blarney Castle** became world famous because Queen Elizabeth I made it a common noun. The castle's owner, Cormac MacCarthy, the Baron of Blarney, incurred the queen's **57** displeasure by his delaying tactics and soothing but evasive chatter. "It's the usual blarney," the queen is said to have despaired. And so tourists climb to the battlement, lie flat on their backs, hang on to two iron bars and extend the head down backwards to kiss the awkwardly placed stone. This may not assure you the gift of the gab, but it could cure your fear of heights.

The castle itself, legends

A mood of yesterday reflected in Cork's river and student's solicitation.

aside, is worth a visit, even if mighty hordes of tourists do besiege it every summer. The formidable square keep was built in the middle of the 15th century. The private park in which the castle is set includes a cool and slightly mysterious dell with ancient occult connections.

In seaports all over the world, ships are seen with *Cobh* written on the stern. You may have wondered where it is and how to say it. **Cobh,** Ireland's biggest south coast port, located 15 miles east of Cork, is pronounced "Cove", which is what it means. But from 1849, when Queen Victoria came to

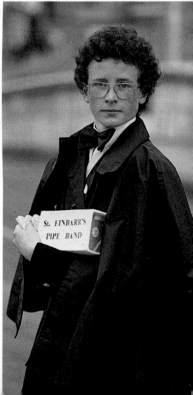

visit, until 1922, it was named Queenstown. The waterfront of this business-like port is washed by waves of nostalgia—for the days of the great transatlantic liners and the earlier, tragic traffic of desperate emigrants fleeing the Irish famine for Canada or the U.S. The old Cunard office is now a bank. On the very steep hill behind the harbour, the gracefully elongated spire of the Catholic **Cathedral of St. Colman** reaches heavenward. In summer, recitals are given on the cathedral's 47-bell carillon.

Youghal (pronounced Yawl) is a popular resort with fully 5 miles of sandy beach and centuries of seafaring history. It's known for its lace, *point d'Irlande.* The town was walled in the Middle Ages, and parts of the fortifications can still be seen. On the site of the main town gate, Youghal's distinctive **Clock Tower** was erected in 1776. The main street runs right through it: the structure's four narrow floors and belfry rise atop an arched platform straddling the street. The tower, now containing the tourist office and a tiny local museum, is an attractive landmark—except for its past. It used to be the municipal jail, and insurrectionists were hanged from the windows to serve as an example to the populace.

Youghal's most impressive monument, **St. Mary's Collegiate Church** (Church of Ireland), is thought to have been founded in the 5th century. Most of the present structure went up in the 13th century, with meticulous restoration in the 19th. Among the lavish monuments and tombs inside the church is one built, in his own honour, by Richard Boyle, a wheeler-dealer of the Elizabethan age who became the first Earl of Cork. A small 17th-century house at the entrance to the churchyard was the occasional home of Sir Walter Raleigh, who once was the mayor of Youghal.

Steep green hills on all sides shelter the tidy port town of **Kinsale,** 18 miles south of Cork. The spacious harbour, virtually landlocked, is a joy to sailors and sightseers alike. For a community of less than 2,000 people, Kinsale has far more than a reasonable share of beauty and historical interest. The town is also renowned for its restaurants, including some of the best in south-east Ireland.

This was the scene of the siege of 1601 in which Spanish troops, who sailed to the aid of the Irish against Queen Elizabeth, took over the town but finally suffered a bitter defeat. It set the stage for the "flight of the Earls", the exodus of the Irish nobility to Europe and the redistribution of their lands. Kinsale became a British naval base.

Nowadays the extravagantly picturesque **harbour** is put to more productive use by fishing boats, sailing dinghies and yachts. Ashore, there are the old **fortifications** to explore, as well as the Norman church of St. Multose, a small castle which held prisoners-of-war until 1800, and a museum containing the first town charter granted by Edward III.

Large colonies of breeding and migratory birds inhabit the dramatic cliffs of the **Old Head** of Kinsale, 10 miles beyond the town. A 20th-century lighthouse here is the successor to a beacon dating back to pre-Christian times. Off the Old Head a German submarine torpedoed the Cunard liner *Lusitania* on May 7, 1915, with the loss of 1,500 lives. The inquest into the disaster was held in the Kinsale Court House.

In West Cork, the town of Bantry is jammed between steep green hills and a bay that looks like a lake. WHIDDY ISLAND, at the head of the bay, was an oil storage depot—until a tanker accident some years ago. The big tankers enjoyed the bay's deep water and sheltering arms—the same advantages which lured invasion forces here in the 17th and 18th centuries. The main sight in **Bantry** itself is Bantry House, a part-Georgian, part-Victorian stately home set in semi-tropical gardens. The tapestries, paintings and furnishing may be viewed on weekdays from April to mid-October.

Heading counter-clockwise around the bay from Bantry, the highway weaves through ever more rocky hills until it descends upon **Glengarriff,** a town to remember. Villas, mansions and simple guest houses all surround themselves with sumptuous gardens made possible by the proximity of the Gulf Stream and the protected southern exposure. Giant eucalyptus, pine and oak trees stand over fuchsia, rhododendron, holly and arbutus. The beauty of the setting and the almost Mediterranean climate account for Glengarriff's year-round popularity.

Ferryboats big and small take visitors through the island-spattered bay from Glengarriff to **Garinish Island,** a 37-acre Eden now run by the National Parks and Monument Service.

The myriad flowers, shrubs and trees come from five continents. Centrepiece of all the horticultural achievement is a walled **Italian garden** surrounding a pool, with the air of some divine perfume factory. In the 19th century Garinish was a bleak military outpost. You can climb to the top of the Martello tower, where sentries once kept a lookout for Napoleonic invasion fleets, and survey the luxuriant hills around the bay.

County Kerry

By any standard this is a spectacular part of the world: the Atlantic in all its moods, lakes designed for lovers or poets, and steep evergreen mountainsides. The inhabitants of the Kingdom of Kerry are special, too—outgoing, generous, perhaps the happy victims of the mysterious spell of their land.

Killarney, the centre of the lakes district, can provide anything the visitor might need, from housing and food to fish-

ing tackle. Seeing the sights is accomplished in an uncommon variety of ways here—by car, coach, bicycle, boat or "jaunting car", a horse-drawn rig driven by a jarvey (guide) who knows the territory and how to tell a story on the way.

Among places to see near Killarney:

Gap of Dunloe and **Lakes of Killarney.** Because of difficult terrain and logistical problems, this is best done on an organized excursion, usually an

Killarney is worth a detour, though reading all those bilingual signs might slow your progress down a bit.

all-day trip. The gap, a wild gorge 4 miles long, can only be traversed on pony-back, in a pony trap, or, if you insist, on foot. Sound-effects underline the weirdness of the rock-strewn scenery as echoes bounce off the mountainsides—to the west, MacGillycuddy's Reeks, the highest **63** range in Ireland; to the east, Purple Mountain. The long trek leads down to the shore of the Upper Lake, where the tour continues by boat. The scenery around the lakes— thick forests, stark crags and enchanted islands—could scarcely be more romantic. But there's adventure, too: shooting the rapids at Old Weir Bridge.

Muckross Abbey. A 15th-century friary with a massive square tower, a cloister with Gothic arches on two sides and Norman or Romanesque on the others and a very old, weathered yew tree in the middle. Muckross House, now a museum of Kerry crafts and folklore, is surrounded by outstanding gardens.

Ross Castle. A 14th-century ruin near old copper mines on a peninsula of the Lower Lake. The castle's garrison surrendered to Cromwell in 1652, awed by an ancient superstition that strange ships spelled

---

Shamrock Curtain

Travelling in the west of Ireland you may suddenly cross the Shamrock Curtain, an invisible cultural frontier. The signs are printed in hard-to-decipher Gaelic letters and the people are talking a cryptic ancient tongue. You've stumbled into the Gaeltacht, pockets of green scattered over seven counties. They make up the main line of resistance to the predominance of that mighty international language, English. The Dublin government actively supports the Gaeltacht efforts to keep the old language and culture alive.

Courses in Irish are offered in the Gaeltacht every summer. If you can't attend, don't be afraid to go into the area. It's quite rare to find anyone who can't also speak English.

64

doom. The attackers knew the legend and brought armed vessels overland from Kinsale.

The **Ring of Kerry** may well be the most sensational 112 miles you ever drove. Set aside a whole day for the circuit so you have enough time to linger over the sublime sights.

The ring passes among hills as steep and round as volca-

Dingle fishermen chat in Gaelic, but most villagers know English, too.

noes on the way to a coast of rugged cliffs and enthralling seascapes. The trip can be made in either direction; here we proceed clockwise.

Leaving Killarney the road goes past the lush lakeland. The first town on the route, KENMARE, is known for its lacemaking and the fish which cram its estuary. North of the small resort of CASTLECOVE, a couple of miles off the main road, are the ruins of **Staigue Fort.** This 2,500-year-

old stronghold is one of Ireland's archaeological wonders—an almost circular structure about 90 feet across with a wall 18 feet high. It predates the invention of cement, of course, so the construction and survival of such an imposing fortification was quite a feat.

Near the village of CAHERDANIEL the old homestead of Daniel O'Connell, "the Liberator", has been restored and made into a museum. Game fishing is the lure for visitors to WATERVILLE, along with the scenery nearby: pitiless granite mountains on one side of the road, green fields and the sea on the other.

A bridge now links **Valentia Island,** with its cliffs and tropical vegetation, to the mainland at PORTMAGEE. The island was the European terminus of the first Atlantic cable (1866), opening telegraphic contact with America. Off Valentia the SKELLIGS ROCKS rise abruptly from the ocean, shrouded with mystery and birds—20,000 pairs of gannets alone.

On the north shore of the peninsula, sheer green hills plunge almost to sea-level and rocky cliffs complete the descent. **Dingle Bay** seems startlingly wide and the Dingle peninsula looks like another country. Between GLENBEIGH

and Killorglin, the head of the bay is almost completely protected from the force of the sea by huge sandbars extending from either shore. **Rossbeigh Strand,** 4 miles of golden sand, is a dream of a beach.

The last town on the ring, KILLORGLIN, saves all its energies for three days in August, a mad pagan pageant called the Puck Fair. A mountain goat presides over round-the-clock festivities.

To the north, **Tralee** (pop. 17,000), the administrative centre of County Kerry, owes its fame to a songwriter named William Mulchinock (1820–64). "The Rose of Tralee" and its author are honoured in a monument in the spacious town park. "Rose" also calls the tune of Tralee's annual festival in September. Girls of Irish descent from many countries compete in a beauty contest whose winner is crowned not Queen of Kerry but Rose of Tralee.

Other than that, Tralee is the gateway to the Dingle peninsula, a most dramatic finger pointing 30 miles into the Atlantic. On the south shore, amidst severe cliffs and rocky coves, a sandbar grows into an arc of beach jutting more than halfway across the bay. **Inch Strand's** 4 miles of soft sand slide gently into the sea. Behind the bathers and suntanners, archaeologists potter about the dunes, where prehistoric inhabitants left meaningful debris.

The small fishing port and resort of **Dingle** claims to be the most westerly town in Europe. From here to land's end all the hamlets are Irish-speaking, part of the Gaeltacht where the traditional language and folklore are conscientiously preserved. This is harsh farming country; old stone walls overrun with shrubs and vines divide skimpy parcels of land. The sheep which graze on even the most precipitous fields have splotches of red or blue dye on their backs to affirm ownership.

The western part of the peninsula is rich territory for archaeologists. In one area alone, the Fahan group consists of more than 400 clochans (beehive-shaped stone huts) plus forts and other ancient structures.

For a spectacular panorama, drive to the summit of **Connor Pass** (altitude 1,500 feet): the sea to the north and south, mountains and lakes east and west. The near-sighted, or fog-bound, can admire the wild fuchsia and heather beside the road.

The West

Limerick

By the time the waters of the Shannon have reached Limerick (pop. 56,000), they have flowed 170 miles through thick and thin: narrow streams and howling rapids, placid lakes and efficient locks. From Limerick, a seaport and industrial centre, they still have another 60 miles to travel through the Shannon estuary to the open Atlantic.

This key position at the meeting of the river and its tidal waters assured the city a long and often violent history. The Danes were first on the scene. Their belligerent policy provoked repeated attacks by the neighbouring native Irish, who finally drove them out. The Anglo-Normans, in turn, captured the place with the unpretentious Irish name of *Luimneach*, meaning Bare Spot. England's King John, who visited Limerick in 1210, ordered the construction of a bridge and a castle. His **castle** survives but most of the town walls, behind which the townsfolk gathered during times of siege, were pulled down in the 18th century to make way for civic expansion.

The most memorable siege

The Shannon

Briefly deviating from our general progress around the coast, here's a leisurely inland foray down the River Shannon. Bird-watchers, flower-spotters, fishermen and swimmers all rave about cruises on the longest river in Ireland, navigable for 140 bucolic miles. If you don't have the time, money or inclination to hire a live-aboard boat, you can still visit the Shannonside attractions by car or bus.

Most of the cruiser-hiring goes on at **Carrick-on-Shannon,** the "capital" of County Leitrim, Ireland's most rural county. Aside from its big marina, Carrick-on-Shannon finds a superlative in the Costelloe Chapel of Main Street. This century-old mausoleum is hailed locally as the world's second-smallest chapel—which may well be the world's second-smallest boast.

Downstream from Carrick, the river runs into Lough Corry, the first of many interconnected lakes in the Shannon basin. Lough Ree, nearly halfway down the river road, is 16 miles long and 7 miles wide at its extreme, big enough so that wind and tides can become a concern. To add to the drama there are uninhabited wooded islands, some sheltering ancient ruins.

The main cross-country roads ford the Shannon at the very central market town of **Athlone.** The crews of barges, cabin cruisers and row-boats stock up on provisions here. Athlone's medieval castle, overlooking the Shannon Bridge, was much fought over for several centuries. A museum has been opened inside its frequently repaired walls.

About 13 miles south of Athlone, at a bend in the river, the ancient monastic settlement of **Clonmacnois** is revealed in a perfect pastoral setting. Founded in the middle of the 6th century by St. Ciaran, the son of a chariot-builder, Clonmacnois grew into a leading medieval university. Because of its low-lying riverside location, it was vulnerable to plunderers, who attacked on many occasions.

The smallest of eight churches here, Temple Ciaran, is thought to contain the founder's grave. West of the temple, the **Cathedral** of Clonmacnois was built in 904 but repaired and expanded over several centuries. It's a modest 62 feet long. In front of the cathedral's west doorway stands the **Cross of the Scriptures,** an unexcelled example of stonecarving about a thousand years old. The illustrations range from biblical scenes to portraits of local dignitaries.

Rocket-shaped O'Rourke's Tower was taller than its present 60 feet **68** before a 12th-century lightning bolt cut off its head. Between the tower and the landward entrance to the compound, gravestones of great antiquity are embedded in a wall.

Back to the river, and 4 miles south of Clonmacnois a 16-arch bridge marks SHANNONBRIDGE, a well-named village with a rambling old fort.

At the village of SHANNON HARBOUR the Grand Canal from Dublin meets the river. The town of PORTUMNA, at the entrance to Lough Derg, is an up-and-coming fishing and boating resort with a new marina. **Lough Derg** is the largest of the Shannon lakes, 25 miles long and up to 3 miles wide. With a full quota of fetching islets and a sky-line of fair green hills beyond, the lake brings the boating to a beauti-ful climax.

Which is just as well, for dangerous rapids await right below the town of **Killaloe,** a prudent place to abandon ship. Killaloe was a great ecclesiastical centre. **St. Flannan's Cathedral** (Church of Ireland) has been restored to its 12th-century glory. The richly carved Romanesque doorway (blocked on the outside) is said to be the entrance to the tomb of King Murtagh O'Brien of Munster (died 1120). The unusual granite shaft nearby, from about the year 1000, bears a bilingual inscription, in Runic and Ogham letters—a foretaste of today's Irish-English road signs.

There once was a cloud-laden sky that glowered but passed by, without wetting the town of Limerick.

was endured after the Battle of the Boyne (1690), when the Irish supporters of James II (see p. 20) retired to Limerick pursued by William of Orange. In spite of heroic efforts, the losers eventually lost again. But the Treaty of Limerick, which permitted the garrison to emigrate with honour, softened the blow further by guaranteeing the Irish freedom of religion. Unfortunately, this was repudiated by the English Parliament, so Limerick claims the melancholy title of City of the Violated Treaty.

Limerick's major historical monument, the 800-year-old **St. Mary's Cathedral** (Church of Ireland), spans many eras of architecture and art. The great square fortress-like tower complements the arched Irish-Romanesque west door. The

15th-century carved **misericords** under the choir seats show a free-ranging imagination, with representations of an angel, an eagle, a goat, a dragon and other such figures in relief. The cathedral grounds form the background for a historical sound-and-light show.

St. John's Catholic Cathedral, in neo-Gothic style, claims the highest spire in Ireland (280 feet tall). Next to the cathedral, major reconstruction and restoration work is reviving St. John's Square, an elegant 18th-century urban ensemble.

The word "limerick", a humorous poem of five lines, probably comes from the refrain "Will you come up to Limerick?", sung as part of a parlour game in which participants had to made up nonsense verse.

Limerick is the first Irish city many visitors see. The proximity of Shannon Airport has reinforced its historic role as a centre of commerce. The airfield, opened in 1945, made its mark in the adventurous days before non-stop transatlantic travel. Nervous passengers waiting for their planes to be refuelled were offered a novel diversion—the chance to buy luxury goods exempt from tax. The world's first duty-free shop grew into a lavish duty-free shopping centre, and the airport became the hub of an industrial development similarly based on tax concessions.

Then the Shannon Free Airport Development Company took over the management of **Bunratty Castle,** and turned it into a thriving tourist attraction. The castle, just a few miles from the airport, has been restored to its original 15th-century atmosphere. It is furnished with wood-carvings and 14th–17th century tapestries and furniture worthy of any museum. At night "Medieval Banquets" are recreated for visitors by professional Irish entertainers in period costumes. Candlelit gluttony is accompanied by the soothing music of the Irish harp.

The latest addition to the Bunratty tourist complex is a **Folk Park** containing replicas of typical old houses of the Shannon region. The peat fires are kept burning, as if the inhabitants had just stepped out to milk a cow or catch a fish.

The administrative centre of County Clare, ENNIS, has a 13th-century **Franciscan friary.** At one time in the Middle Ages it had 350 friars and 600 students. The buildings, expanded and revamped over the centuries, were finally renovated in the 1950s.

The Burren

North-west of Ennis, more than 200 square miles of County Clare belongs to the Burren, a zone of bizarre geological developments. Glaciers and erosion have created limestone "pavements", horizontal slabs divided by fissures that look like the legacy of an earthquake. Though a moonscape is sometimes suggested, the Burren is anything but barren; it is a quiet world of small animals, birds, butterflies and even flowers of the Mediterranean species. At first glance the area might seem hostile to human habitation, but the profusion of megalithic tombs and forts proves that it has supported a population for many centuries. While geologists, botanists and archaeologists are having a field day atop the "pavements", speleologists are enjoying the Burren's caves. More than 25 miles of caves have been explored here. Most are for experts only, but anyone can visit Aillwee Cave southeast of BALLYVAUGHAN (open April to October).

In KILFENORA, a village on the edge of this carboniferous limestone plain, the citizens have established the informative **Burren Display Centre,** a quick pleasant way to get your Burren bearings. Kilfenora Cathedral, founded in the 12th century, is noted for its interesting sculptured monuments. The village is over-endowed with carved high crosses.

The **Cliffs of Moher,** 6 miles north-west of LAHINCH, rise nearly 700 feet above the Atlantic. From O'Brien's Tower, a 19th-century observation post near the edge, the spectacle moves the spirit: the cliff-faces just stand there above the sea posing for pictures, the horizontal layers as easily defined as the storeys of a glass skyscraper. You watch a great wave crash against the foot of the cliff but the thump is heard a little late, like the report of a distant artillery shell. Thousands of sea birds—razorbills, puffins, kittiwakes, gulls—live along the cliffs.

The Burren town of **Lisdoonvarna** is famous as a spa with overtones of romance. The local springs produce mineral waters rich in sulphur, iron and iodine, thought to be good for rheumatic conditions and as a general tonic. Though not apparently romantic in itself, the town has acquired a reputation as a match-making mec-

Momentarily calm, the Atlantic lies in wait along the Cliffs of Moher.

A seascape for poets at Lahinch Strand. Opposite: waiting for the Aran fishing boats to come home.

ca. For generations, spinsters and bachelors from all over the country have come to Lisdoonvarna in a final attempt to find a mate, making Ireland's first spa their last resort. Recently, folk music festivals in the area have broadened the appeal, and lowered the average age at the local dances.

Just across the border in County Galway, the area around the town of GORT has powerful literary associations. Lady Gregory, co-founder of the Abbey Theatre, lived in **Coole Park,** now a national forest. The "autograph tree" there is inscribed with the initials of some of her visitors—Augustus John, John Masefield, Sean O'Casey and one of the few authors instantly recognized by his initials, George Bernard Shaw.

Four miles north-east of Gort, William Butler Yeats bought a 16th-century tower, **Thoor Ballylee,** as inspiring a place as any poet could pick for a home. Visitors may wander around the romantic tower with its spiral staircase, secretive alcoves and, right out the window, its own burbling stream.

Galway

The main city of the western province of Connaught, Gal-way (pop. 48,000) is a port, resort, administrative and cultural centre. In the Middle Ages it prospered as a sort of city-state but withered after two 17th-century disasters: prolonged sieges by the forces of Cromwell and, four decades later, by William of Orange. Relics of the old glory still glimmer in corners of the renewed city.

The **Collegiate Church of St. Nicholas** (Church of Ireland) was begun by the Anglo-

Normans in 1320. According to local tradition, Christopher Columbus worshipped there before setting out on his voyage of discovery to America. The locals like to think Columbus was checking out the details of the 6th-century transatlantic explorer, St. Brendan. A pyramid steeple tops this triple-naved church, full of fine stone-carvings and statuary.

During Galway's heyday 14 families, mostly of Welsh and Norman descent, formed a sort of medieval Mafia that controlled the economic and political life of the town. Their great common enemy, the O'Flaherty family, inspired the inscription (1549) over the old town gate: "From the fury of the O'Flaherties, good Lord deliver us." Of Galway's 14 "tribes", the Lynches left the most memories and monuments.

Lynch's Castle, a townhouse of around 1600, is decorated with excellent stonework —coats-of-arms, gargoyles and carved window-frames. This rare building, lovingly restored, now houses a bank.

Another Lynch reminder is the "Lynch Memorial Window" with a plaque recounting the macabre story of James Lynch FitzStephen, mayor of Galway in 1493, who condemned and executed his own son, Walter, for murder. Judge Lynch became the hangman when nobody else in town would agree to serve. If this, as widely thought, inspired the expression "lynch law", it must be a madly devious derivation; the crowd didn't lynch young Lynch but wanted to save him.

Galway's Catholic cathedral—officially the Cathedral of Our Lady Assumed into Heaven and St. Nicholas—has a giant dome looming over the city. The mainly classical architecture might be misleading; the church was dedicated in 1965.

Alongside the cathedral is one of Galway's most celebrated sights; the **Salmon Weir.** Through this watery bottleneck the salmon fight their way from the sea up to Galway's lakeland. At certain times of year (June–July) you can see them queueing up for a chance to leap above the falls and follow their instincts to sweet water.

Galway's seaside suburb, **Salthill,** is a big, popular resort with rocky seawalls and beaches of fine sand. It's a good place to watch the sun go down on Galway Bay; sprawling hills enclose almost all of this immense bay, but the Atlantic can be seen and sensed to the west.

Connemara and the Aran Islands

Lough Corrib, extending 27 miles north from Galway, is big enough to be whipped by waves when a sudden wind hurtles down the hillside. It's generally shallow and well supplied with islands and fish—salmon, trout, pike and perch. Lake Corrib divides County Galway into two contrasting regions: to the east is a fertile limestone plain; to the west Connemara, with dramatic mountains, a sprinkling of lakes and an Atlantic coastline of fjords and pristine beaches.

Much of Connemara is an Irish-speaking enclave. This is the home of the Connemara pony—compact, robust, intelligent and self-reliant. Spanish horses of the 16th century are said to have cross-bred with Irish ponies; one version says the stallions swam ashore from ships of the Spanish Armada wrecked on nearby rocks.

The sky seems to change by the minute in the far west—dazzling sun, fleeting clouds and rain alternating so quickly that photographers have to keep changing readings. But the pictures are worth the trouble in this land of thatched white cottages and 180-degree rainbows.

The so-called capital of Connemara, the well-placed market town of **Clifden,** is a good base for explorations of nearby lakes, rivers, beaches, bogs and mountains. Clifden's Irish name is *An Clochan*, meaning the Stepping-Stones. There are so many bodies of water around Clifden that you can't tell the sea inlets from the

From Bog to Stove

In an energy-hungry world it sounds too good to be true: go out in a field, dig up the moist topsoil, dry it, then burn it for cooking, heating the house, even generating electricity. In real life it's not so easy, but peat, the typically Irish fuel, does produce about half the heat of coal.

Locally known as turf, peat is found in the bogs which cover one-sixth of the country. It is created by centuries of interaction between the bog's water and vegetable matter. After the bog is drained, the turf is cut into uniform chunks (see photo opposite), stacked for drying, and eventually collected for use. A typical family burns 12 to 15 tonnes a year.

And now city slickers can buy peat briquettes to burn in their fireplaces for the sweet nostalgic smell of Ireland.

coves of the lakes except for the seaweed.

Killary Harbour, near LEE-NANE, is a superb anchorage protected by high mountain walls on both sides. The floats and rafts which look as if they belong to an oil exploration project are actually busy farming mussels. The Irish don't think much of seafood so they're exported to enthusiastic French clients.

The **Twelve Bens** of Connemara (*ben* is Gaelic for peak) constitute a range of moody mountains inhabited mostly by sheep; the verdant foothills are interspersed with bogs and pretty lakes.

And now for some real escapism. Out in the Atlantic, 30 miles off Galway, the **Aran Islands** are a last bastion of peace and quiet and unbroken tradition. Their tall, handsome people, with strong, open faces, survive on a land so harsh that every blade of grass seems a miracle. They raise cattle, catch fish, and spin, weave and knit. Aran sweaters are sold all over Ireland but only here can you be sure it's the genuine, hand-made article.

Inishmore, "the Big Island" as the Aran folk call it, is about 9 miles from tip to tip and 2 miles across. From the air—and you can fly there from

Galway—it's a tight gridwork of stone fences enclosing small boxes of meagre pasturage. In some fields you can see the bare rock beneath the grass. Inishmore's only real village, KILRONAN, has a well-protected fishing port where ferryboats from the mainland dock. The fishermen work aboard modern trawlers, but the traditional *currachs* are still used, too. These tar-coated, canvas-hulled boats, made by hand, now enjoy the power of outboard motors.

Seagulls celebrate a fishing boat's exploits. Ashore: cleaning the catch.

This is an island to explore on foot or rented bicycle. If you're in a hurry, pony-traps are available for guided tours. The island even has a motorized taxi which doubles as a school bus.

Inishmore's most remarkable monument is **Dun Aengus,** a giant prehistoric fortress balanced on the sheer edge of a cliff 300 feet high. It's a 15-minute walk from the nearest road, across unobtrusively marked fields. Three layers of stone walls, the outermost 20 feet high, surround a courtyard 150 feet across. With all the ramparts and obstacles set up beyond the wall, the defensive area covers 11 acres. Even in modern times it would take a rash general to attack Dun Aengus.

Elsewhere on the islands, amidst wild flowers, wandering sheep and cows and an abundance of bounding rabbits, there are many lesser archaeological sites: more forts, primitive stone dwellings, hermits' cells called beehive huts, round towers and ruined churches.

In striking contrast to these and other traditional structures, a big glass-walled factory in the west of Inishmore exports its production to many corners of the world. The time-honoured dexterity of the Aran women has been diverted from wool to wire; the employees weave telephone cable and make electronic components. The language they all speak is Irish.

But most people on the islands can also express themselves in English. Whether they say "Failte" or "Welcome", they have a friendly greeting for strangers.

County Mayo

Rising high above Clew Bay, a few miles south-west of Westport, **Croagh Patrick** is Ireland's Holy Mountain. In a country of the most appealing green mountains, the holy peak happens to look like a thoroughly forbidding black slag heap. Nonetheless, thousands of pilgrims—some barefoot—climb the hostile, gravelly slopes to the 2,510-foot summit where St. Patrick is said to have spent Lent in 441. There are inspiring views of the island-speckled bay and the hills of counties Mayo, Clare and Galway.

The town of **Westport,** at the head of Clew Bay, is a dignified example of late 18th-century urban planning. A tree-lined boulevard called the Mall follows the channeled Carrowbeg River, and the town's main plaza is an elegant octagon.

Just outside the town, the stately home of the Marquess of Sligo may be toured from April to October. The rooms of **Westport House** are as palatial as you would expect, and the paintings, silver and glassware are notable. There's a souvenir shop, pinball machines, go-carts for children, and even a dungeon.

Inland, the village of **Knock** (from the Irish *Cnoc Mhuire*—Mary's Hill) ranks with Lourdes or Fátima as a place of pilgrimage. In 1879 townsfolk saw an apparition of the Virgin Mary, St. Joseph and St. John on the south gable of the old parish church. The centenary year reached a climax when a pilgrim from Rome, Pope John Paul II, addressed an open-air mass at Knock attended by at least 400,000 of the faithful.

Getting there is easy now that the international airport is in operation.

A new **basilica**—Ireland's biggest church—had been built in advance of the anniversary; it can hold 20,000 worshippers. The small parish church is still there, but the **south gable** had to be restored after much of the mortar was taken away as relics. The site of the apparition has been enclosed in glass, and white marble statues re-create the position of the figures in the vision.

Knock is a one-industry town catering to the pilgrims. Many shops sell religious souvenirs. There is also a museum of folklore and handicrafts.

Achill, Ireland's biggest island is buffeted by wind and tide; meagre farms huddle between ominous mountain and rocky shore. It feels adrift in the Atlantic, even though you can drive there from the mainland over a relatively short and unimpressive bridge.

Driving on Achill's wide-open, almost deserted roads revives the joy of motoring. But even if the traffic were heavy, the scenery—from 800-foot cliffs to superb beaches —would be worth the trouble.

Near the village of KEEL, **Trawmore Strand** is an outstanding model of a sweeping white-sand beach. Keel's 9-hole golf course, spreading to the dunes, suffers no shortage of sand traps.

Prehistoric graves are found on the slopes of Achill's overpowering mountain, the 2,204-foot Slievemore. Ocean drives offer dizzying **cliff views** and perspectives over an ocean churning round off-islands and shoals. Inland, three-chimneyed white cottages nestle between moors and bogs.

83

The North-West

Sligo (pop. 18,000) lies at the end of a well-protected harbour, snug between the silhouettes of two mountains of great character, Ben Bulben and Knocknarea. It's a busy industrial and commercial centre but small enough for strangers on the street to be greeted with a shy smile and a tilt of the head that means hello.

Early fame came to Sligo in 807 when the Vikings overran the place. In 1252 Maurice Fitzgerald, Earl of Kildare, founded **Sligo Abbey**, a Dominican friary. It was accidentally burned down in 1414 but rebuilt soon after. Finally the abbey was sacked by Puritan troops in 1641; all the friars are believed to have been shot or burned to death. The ruins standing today mark a curious convergence of desolation and grace. Three sides of the **cloister** have been preserved, and there are bits of excellent stone-carving.

The resort of **Strandhill,** west of Sligo, has a vast, easy-sloping sand beach prone to receive long-rolling waves which delight surfers. **Knocknarea,** the flat-topped mountain hanging over this stretch of shore, must have had a strange attraction for prehistoric settlers. The area is abundantly supplied with megalithic monuments and on the 1,078-foot summit of Knocknarea is a huge **cairn** (tomb of stones). Legend says it is the burial place of the first-century Queen Maeve of Connaught.

Facing Strandhill on the opposite side of the harbour, **Rosses Point** is a quiet family resort with miles of beaches. And between the two lies CONEY ISLAND, an almost uninhabited island after which, it is said, New York's amusement park was named.

W.B. Yeats is buried exactly as he specified in a poem completed shortly before his death in 1939: "Under bare Ben Bulben's head in Drumcliff churchyard". The **grave** is near the front door of the town's small church, with its turreted belfry rising in the very shadow of the awesome mountain. **Ben Bulben,** 1,730 feet high, hangs over the countryside like a great green aircraft carrier. On the flat top unusual arctic and alpine plants are found.

Seventeen miles north of Sligo, on the approaches to the beach resort and fishing village of MULLAGHMORE, the century-old Classiebawn Castle has the skyline all to itself. This was the summer home of Earl Mountbatten of Burma; he was assassinated in 1979 when his fishing boat was blown up just offshore.

County Donegal

The most northerly county on the island, Donegal is best known for the great variety of scenery—seascapes and lakes, mountains and glens. Rocky hills support nimble-hooved cows and confident sheep, and the coast is studded with pretty ports and hidden beaches. This is where the famous Donegal homespun tweeds come from.

DONEGAL TOWN's most imposing building, a 15th-century **castle,** occupies the site of a previous Viking fort. (*Dun na nGall* in Irish means the Fortress of the Foreigners, evidently a reference to the Vikings.) On the outskirts of town, the 15th-century ruins of Donegal Abbey overlook the estuary.

Westward along the coast, KILLYBEGS is a really big-time fishing port; the trawlers have wheelhouses like space-age control rooms with electronic devices to track down the big schools.

The road to **Glencolumbkille** undulates through spectacular mountain-and-seascape country. At last, coming over the crest of a hill, you see the simple village far below, enfolded in green hillsides that funnel down to the sea. Glencolumbkille means the Glen of St. Colmcille, otherwise known as St. Columba. It is suggested that the 6th-century saint, who changed history by bringing Christianity to Scotland, began his career by converting the locals. Many ancient **standing-stones** in the glen may have been pagan monuments which Columba adapted to the new religion. On the saint's feast day, June 9, pilgrims follow the route of these stones, perhaps in Columba's footsteps. Throughout the glen more than 40 prehistoric dolmens, souterrains and cairns have been catalogued, some as ancient as 5,000 years old.

Northern Ireland

The Union Jack flies over six of the nine counties of the ancient province of Ulster, a fact which stirs the most fiery feelings. Unarguably, the "sectarian violence" of recent years has affected daily life in Northern Ireland: the centre of Belfast has been turned into a pedestrian mall by default, surrounded by a stern security cordon. But the scenery of exuberant hills, lovely lakes and **85** a grandiose seacoast remains unscathed. Here is a brief rundown of the most imperative Northern attractions:

The Glens of Antrim. The Antrim Coast Road, a marvel of 19th-century engineering, hugs the most scenic coast, beneath white cliffs, beside beaches, through quaint villages and among rocks which summarize the geological history of our planet. The seascapes may be splendid but the nine idyllic glens along the way, with forests and waterfalls, are the stuff legends are made of.

The Giant's Causeway. One of the candidates for "eighth wonder of the world," this is

Northern Ireland's most awe-inspiring sight, the famous Giant's Causeway.

Ireland's most amazing natural phenomenon. Molten lava was frozen into some 38,000 basalt columns, mostly hexagonal, which form tightly packed "stepping stones" out into the sea. Such a vast and spectacular oddity, 60 million years old, excites the imagination; individual formations have names like the Honeycomb, the Chimney Pots and the Wishing Chair. Nearby at PORT NA SPANIAGH, a ship of the Spanish Armada was wrecked in 1588. Nearly four centuries later Belgian divers recovered a king's ransom in gold, silver and jewels. The best pieces are now on view at the Ulster Museum in Belfast.

The Lakes of Fermanagh. Ulster's indefatigable statisticians can't say how many lakes County Fermanagh actually contains, but they have counted 154 islands in the 50-mile stretch of Upper and Lower Lough Erne. "Fisherman's paradise" is the usual subtitle for Fermanagh, and no wonder. In 1979, an angler named Dennis Willis pulled in 207 pounds in five hours. Millions more roach, pike, perch and bream are still available, and there is no closed season on coarse fishing.

The Mourne Mountains. In Northern Ireland's highest range, compact but aloof, 15 granite hills rise higher than 2,000 feet. On the summit of Slieve Donard are two cairns—ancient mounds of stones. From here, on a flawless day, you can see Scotland, England, the Isle of Man and Snowdonia in Wales.

Ulster Folk and Transport Museum. Much livelier than its name might indicate, this institution enjoys 172 acres of woodland park. Old farmhouses, mills and a church were moved stone by stone from their original sites all over Ulster to preserve in one spot the agricultural, industrial and social history of the province. In the new transport section you can admire ancient carriages, bicycles, cars and aircraft. This museum, at Cultra Manor, Holywood, County Down, is about 8 miles from central Belfast.

The modern **Ulster Museum,** in Belfast itself, also looks out onto a park, the Botanic Gardens. The museum's art department features Irish and British painting up to the present day. Archaeological exhibits begin with prehistoric Irish artefacts and continue to working relics of the Industrial Revolution which transformed Belfast from a village to a metropolis.

What to Do

Sports

By land and by sea (and river and lake) the Irish enjoy sporting possibilities so comprehensive that we can only touch on a handful of favourites. But if you're interested in more esoteric sports such as hang-gliding, orienteering or polo—the tourist board can put you in touch with the relevant associations.

Water Sports

Sailing. Old salts with seaworthy yachts welcome the challenges off the west coast but less expert sailors can handle conditions off the south and east coasts and in bays all around the island. Ask the tourist board for literature on boat hire and sailing tuition, giving addresses and prices.

Sea fishing. Any way you like it—from a sandy beach, a pier, a clifftop or a boat—you can hook big beautiful trophies of the deep: shark, sea bass, tope, skate, halibut, conger...

Swimming. The Irish Tourist Board's information sheet on seaside resorts lists an even 12 dozen—not bad for a modestly sized island. The beaches come in all shapes and sizes but they have this in common: no crowds.

Surfing. Atlantic swells are more impressive on the west and north coasts.

On the lakes and rivers:

Game fishing. The most fertile salmon fisheries are restricted but arrangements can be made—preferably well in advance. Trout are abundant in rivers and lakes, with some minor restrictions. Sea trout invade rivers and lakes; as in the case of salmon, a licence is required.

Coarse fishing. Free for all, almost everywhere, all year round, with outsize takings in bream, pike, roach, perch, etc.

Boating. Cruising on the Shannon or lesser Irish rivers is a popular vacation in itself. For the more energetic, canoeing on placid lakes, or rivers either relaxing or rough.

Sports Ashore

Golf. In a country so green, you scarcely notice the golf courses, but there are about 200, including several of championship status. Non-members

88

Easy-going lake fishing and undersea expeditions show the variety of water sport available in Ireland.

are sometimes excluded on weekends, but you'll have no problems on Monday to Friday. And between rounds you can keep in shape with pitch and putt, an Irish game that's somewhere between minigolf and the real thing, played with a putter and one other club.

Horse riding. Stables all over Ireland have fine Irish horses, beautiful ponies, and plans for treks through delightful countryside. Instruction is available.

Hunting and shooting. Foxhunts and game shooting have many enthusiasts in Ireland. Best to make advance inquiries through the tourist authorities.

Tennis. Many hotels have their own courts, some with instructors. Elsewhere there are public courts, as in many Dublin parks.

Spectator Sports

Horse racing. Almost everyone in Ireland seems to be engrossed in the Sport of Kings, one way or another. Dublin has two tracks, and several well-known courses are within

Ducks on sale in Kilkenny are designed to decoy shoppers. At Bunratty Folk Park, opposite, old Irish handicrafts are demonstrated to visitors.

easy day-trip distance. The flat season runs from March to November; steeple-chase racing goes on all year.

Greyhound racing. Harebrained dogs keep the punters busy six nights a week in Dublin, which has two greyhound stadiums, and elsewhere.

National games. Hurling is a lightning-fast variant on hockey; a small leather-covered ball is struck, on the ground or in the air, by a "hurley", resembling a hockey stick. Gaelic football, the other distinctively Irish game, contains elements of soccer and rugby.

Imported games. Soccer, rugby, athletics and even cricket are widely played.

Shopping

Friendly, low-keyed sales personnel help make shopping in Ireland such a pleasure. Shopkeepers and assistants are full of informed advice, and so sincere they're likely to advertise a competitor if they think he's selling something better or cheaper.

The most appealing products here are made by Irish craftsmen in traditional or imaginative new styles. Some ideas for shoppers, in alphabetical order:

Aran sweaters. The elaborate stitches in this fisherman's sweater, knitted of undyed wool, can easily be recognized. Demand so far exceeds the supply that they are made in mainland factories as well as in the cottages of the islands of their origin. Be sure to examine the label to find out whether the Aran sweater, scarf or cap is hand-knit.

Connemara marble, rich green in colour, made into bookends, bracelets and brooches.

Crosses. Especially reproductions of ancient Christian crosses, and St. Brigid crosses of straw.

Dolls, dressed in traditional regional costumes.

Enamel dishes, plaques and pendants by local craftsmen.

Fishing flies from Donegal and Tipperary.

Glassware. Waterford crystal, world renowned until the industry succumbed to 19th-century economic pressures, is again a going concern.

Jewellery. Ancient Celtic designs and illustrations from the Book of Kells inspire some of today's goldsmiths and silversmiths.

Kinsale smocks. Stylish cotton wind-cheaters for sailors. Not to be confused with Kinsale cloaks, traditional local dress now revived as chic evening-wear.

Lace. Convents in Limerick and County Monaghan have kept this industry alive.

Linen. Weaving goes on in Northern Ireland but the finished product—from handkerchiefs to table sets—is sold everywhere.

Peat. The turf of Ireland is now compressed and sculpted into reproductions of ancient religious and folklore symbols.

Pottery. Traditional and modern designs in tableware and ovenware.

Records. Individuals and groups sing or play traditional tunes.

Rushwork. In this land of thatched cottages, the makers of woven baskets and similar wickerwork are still in business.

Smoked salmon. The souvenir you can eat is specially packed for travelling, on sale at the airport. So are Irish sausages, and butter, if it comes to that.

Tweed. Handwoven Irish fabrics now come in a considerable variety of colours and weights, fit for winter overcoats or light shawls or drapes.

Whimsical souvenirs. Leprechauns in all sizes, "worry stones" of marble, Irish coffee glasses and shillelaghs (cudgels).

A Way with Words

Story-telling just comes naturally to the Irish. How else can you explain this small country's substantial contribution to world literature? Here, in chronological order, are nine of the greatest.

Jonathan Swift (1667–1745), dean of satirists, was also the dean of St. Patrick's Cathedral, Dublin. Writing was only a part-time job for the romantic clergyman best remembered for *Gulliver's Travels*.

Oliver Goldsmith (c. 1728–74). Son of a clergyman, he studied medicine, entered the London circle of Dr. Samuel Johnson and wrote the novel *The Vicar of Wakefield*, the play *She Stoops to Conquer* and the poem *The Deserted Village*.

Richard Brinsley Sheridan (1751–1816), the writer of three famous stage comedies—*The Rivals, The School for Scandal* and *The Critic*— later turned to politics. After a career in the British House of Commons he died in poverty.

Oscar Wilde (1854–1900). His haunting novel, *The Picture of Dorian Gray*, was followed by witty London comedies like *The Importance of Being Earnest*. Imprisoned on a charge of homosexual conduct, he was inspired to write *The Ballad of Reading Gaol*.

George Bernard Shaw (1856–1950), Dublin-born, spent most of his life in England. *Arms and the Man, Man and Superman* and *Pygmalion* made him the greatest dramatist of the age. Shaw also kept in the public eye as an inveterate controversialist.

William Butler Yeats (1865–1939), like Shaw, won the Nobel prize. His poems sang the glories of the Irish land, legends and heroes. He was a founder of the Abbey Theatre and served as a senator of the young Irish Free State.

John Millington Synge (1871–1909). Like Swift, Goldsmith and Wilde, he was educated at Trinity College, Dublin. His plays *Riders to the Sea* and *The Playboy of the Western World* are part of Abbey Theatre history.

Sean O'Casey (1880–1964), another Abbey monument, wrote brilliant tragi-comedy—*The Shadow of a Gunman, Juno and the Paycock* and *The Plough and the Stars*. His later plays, stronger on ideological rhetoric, were less successful.

James Joyce (1882–1941) re-created Dublin in his imagination from the vantage point of European exile. *Ulysses*, his revolutionary stream-of-consciousness novel in a Homeric framework, was banned in Ireland (and elsewhere) during his lifetime.

Nightlife

Many hotels and pubs present **cabaret nights** featuring a cross-section of distinctively Irish entertainment: folksingers, harpists, dancers and storytellers. In some local pubs the programme might consist of a lone folksinger with guitar. At the other end of the scale, the luxury hotels put on elaborate productions with a platoon of performers.

The shows have a typically Irish mixture of hand-clapping high spirits and "Come Back to Erin" nostalgia. Light-footed lasses tirelessly dance jigs and reels, tap dancers revive old routines. Harps and banjoes are plucked, bagpipes and accordions are squeezed. Fiddlers are as ubiquitous as the gypsy violinists of Budapest, though a lot more cheerful.

You will find less highly polished versions of traditional Irish music at *fleadhanna*, festivals of music and song around the country, climaxing in the All Ireland *Fleadh* in August. Tourist offices have schedules.

Restored medieval castles are used for another kind of night out—**banquets** by candlelight with traditional stories, poems and songs, tragic or bawdy. These re-creations of lusty celebrations in centuries past are professionally arranged and executed. Visitors without cars can sign on to package tours which include door-to-door transportation.

Ireland's great **theatrical** tradition—which gave the world Goldsmith, Sheridan, Shaw, O'Casey, Beckett and Behan—flickers on in several major

towns, most notably Dublin, Belfast and Cork. The Abbey Theatre of Dublin, in a new modern home, is still "packing them in" after more than 75 years.

The newspapers give full listings of theatrical happenings as well as concerts (pop and classical) and films.

Festivals and Special Events

March: St. Patrick's Week, parades and other events in Dublin and various towns.

April: Dublin Arts Festival—concerts, plays, exhibitions.

May: Cork International Cho-

ral and Folk Dance Festival.

Dublin Spring Show and Industries Fair.

Killarney Pan-Celtic Week, competitions and cultural events with participation from other Celtic countries.

June: Festival of Music in Great Irish Houses, with the setting as grand as the celebrity of the performers.

City of Dublin International Festival of Music—competitions for bands, groups and solo performers.

July: Cobh International Folk Dance Festival.

August: Dublin Horse Show, the top sporting and social event of the year.

September: Rose of Tralee International Festival.

Waterford International Festival of Light Opera, a unique musical event.

October: Dublin Theatre Festival—new plays by Irish authors and visiting companies from Europe and America.

Cork International Film Festival.

Wexford Opera Festival, featuring rare operas and talented performers.

November: Dublin Indoor International Horse Show, another classic of the Royal Dublin Society and one of the major events on the international equestrian calendar.

Dining and Drinks

Like most Anglo-Saxons, the Irish prefer "honest" meat and potatoes heaped high on their plates. Not for them the esoteric sauces and spices of European cuisines. In Ireland if you ask someone to recommend a restaurant the criterion is likely to be quantity, not quality.

Even so, you can hardly go wrong when it comes to the ingredients. The abundance of fresh meat, fish, butter and eggs goes a long way to compensate for the lack of *haute cuisine* in most Irish restaurants.

Meals are served in a somewhat baffling variety of establishments—hotels, bars, coffee shops, snack bars, pubs...and even restaurants. "Pub grub" tends to be meat pies, sandwiches and simple salads. Restaurants run from the most modest to truly elegant, with prices to match. There are ever more foreign restaurants, especially in the big towns.

Keep in mind the "businessman's lunch", a package deal found in many restaurants, usually involving three courses for a fraction of the cost of the evening meal.

In addition to VAT (value-added tax), a lot of restaurants add a service charge to the bill; extra tips are rare.

When to Eat
Breakfast is served from about 7 to 10 a.m., though in some hotels, matching the general leisurely air, it doesn't begin until 8. Lunch time runs from 12.30 to 2.30, give or take half an hour at either end. The hour—and name—of the evening meal depends on where and who you are. In country districts and unsophisticated quarters of big towns, people dine as early as 6 p.m. and call dinner, "tea". But in the big towns you can have your supper anytime from 6 or 7 to 11 p.m.

Breakfast
A real Irish breakfast starts the day superlatively. You'll feel ready for all manner of exertion after a menu of juice, porridge or cold cereal with milk or cream, fried eggs with bacon *and* sausages, toast and home-made soda bread, butter, marmalade, tea or coffee. Irish soda bread, white or brown, is made of flour, buttermilk, bicarbonate of soda and salt; it's as delicious as cake.

The Irish prefer unsophisticated, filling meals to "fancy" foreign food.

Lunch and Dinner

Irish **soups** are usually thick and hearty: vegetables and barley and meat stock and a dab of cream, for instance. Look for potato soup made of potatoes, onions, carrot and parsley.

Fish fresh from the Atlantic or the Irish Sea or the island's streams is sensationally good. The Irish, however, lack interest in almost all kinds of seafood, presumably because of a mental block—until recent years Catholics were obliged to abstain from meat on Fridays, so fish was thought of as a poor substitute. Keep an eye out for these great Irish delights: fresh salmon (poached or grilled), smoked salmon, sole, trout from sea or stream. Dublin Bay prawns are a worthily famous natural resource, as are Galway oysters (often washed down with a bottle of stout). With luck you'll be offered local mussels or lobster, though the great bulk of the catch is exported to appreciative clients on the Continent.

Meat of the highest quality is the centre-piece of Irish cuisine. The beef is excellent but there is little veal. You'll have a choice of sumptuous steaks (T-bone, sirloin or filet mignon) or roast beef. Lamb appears in tender chops or roast or as the main ingredient in Irish stew, a filling casserole with potatoes, carrots, onions, parsley and thyme. Irish pork products—bacon, sausages, chops, Limerick ham—are also famous. Dublin Coddle is a stew of bacon, sausages, onions, potatoes and parsley, a favourite Saturday night supper in the capital.

Vegetables as basic as potatoes and cabbage play a big role in Irish cooking. Potatoes have been a mainstay of the Irish diet since the 17th century. Mushrooms, which thrive in the cool and humid atmosphere, are Ireland's biggest horticultural export.

Desserts are often similar to English "puddings"—trifles, gateaux and generally very sweet sweets, often fruity, with a scrumptious topping of thick sweet cream.

Drinks

A pitcher of tap water is frequently found on the table. For many diners it's the only beverage drunk during the meal. Others choose milk. However, wine is becoming much more popular in Ireland as European links strengthen. By an illogical

Wholesome homey cakes and rolls make tea-time a highlight of the day.

quirk in the law, most restaurants licensed to serve sherry and wines are forbidden to serve spirits or beer. And in any case, the Irish consider beer a pub pastime, not a dinner companion.

Irish pubs are usually as relaxed and friendly as the regular clients. But don't forget about the eccentric licensing hours under which public houses in the Republic's urban areas have to close between 2.30 and 3.30 p.m.; and pub hours are drastically reduced on Sundays (in Northern Ireland, totally eliminated).

The Irish drink nearly 500 million pints of beer a year, mostly a rich creamy dark-brown version, stout. In many a pub the laconic order, "A pint, please", means 568 millilitres of Guinness, lovingly drawn from the keg and

Pubs, often steeped in atmosphere, play a key role in community life.

scraped and topped. The "head" is so thick the barman can sculpt it with his spatula like a baker icing a cake. "A glass" of stout means half a pint. Irish lagers and ales, much less filling, are also worth trying. A strange Irish drink, Black Velvet, combines stout and champagne; it is said to be helpful in the event of a hangover.

The word whiskey is derived from the Gaelic *uisce beatha*, "water of life". (Purists must remember to spell Irish whiskey with an "e", unlike Scotch.) Pot-stilled Irish whiskey is matured in wooden casks for at least seven years. It's drunk neat or with a little water. Never with ice. History enthusiasts can visit the world's oldest whiskey distillery, Bushmills, in Northern Ireland—licensed since 1609.

Whiskey figures in some unusual derivative drinks: Irish Coffee, served in a stemmed glass, consists of hot coffee laced with whiskey and sugar with a tablespoonful of thick cream floating on top. Two Irish liqueurs merit a try: Irish Mist—honey and herbs in a whiskey base—tingles the palate, and Irish Cream Liqueur contains whiskey, chocolate and cream, like a leprechaun's milkshake.

Who's Who in Fairyland

Don't laugh at the "Little People" of Irish folklore. Even if you don't believe in fairies, it's safer not to test your luck. Here's the cast of semi-supernatural characters, just in case you meet some of them.

Banshee. Beware: the piercing wail of this silver-haired fairy signals a death; but she means well.

Cluricaun. Look for silver buckles on the shoes of this somewhat boozy night-person.

Far darrig (meaning red man). Dressed in red, he makes mischief, especially black humour at its most terrifying.

Leprechaun. Small pipe-smoking shoemaker, helpful to Irish housewives, a miser of great wealth, most notorious of the "solitary fairies".

Pooka. Is it a bird, a bull or a goat? The only eyewitnesses were drunk at the time, so evidence is hazy.

Sociable, or trooping fairies. As opposed to all the solitaries, listed above, these generally gentle, amiable creatures keep themselves apart from humankind. One character flaw: they sometimes steal children! But fire or holy water are good safeguards.

BLUEPRINT for a Perfect Trip

How to Get There

It is advisable to consult a travel agent for the latest information on tariffs and other arrangements.

From Great Britain

BY AIR: You can fly from airports across the U.K. to Dublin, Shannon, Cork, Waterford and Knock in Ireland. New routes are opening all the time, so check with the airline of your choice for information on the most convenient connections to Ireland.

Charter Flights and Package Tours: A wide array of packages is currently available, including stays at Irish cottages or farmhouses, driving a horse-drawn caravan, river-cruising, self-catering, etc. Some airlines offer fly-drive arrangements, and special fares which include flight plus transport to and from the final destination in Ireland.

BY SEA: Passenger and car ferries sail frequently from Holyhead to Dun Laoghaire and Liverpool to Dublin. There is also a service from Fishguard and Pembroke to Rosslare Harbour, and from Pembroke and Swansea to Cork. Ferries shuttle several times a day from Cairnryan and Stanraer to Larne (near Belfast) and less frequently between Liverpool and Belfast.

Those planning to tour Ireland without a car might want to buy a rambler ticket (8 or 15 days of unlimited bus and rail travel) or an overlander ticket (15 days of bus and rail travel, including Northern Ireland). These tickets can be bought at home or in Ireland from Bus Eireann or Iarnród Eireann-Irish Rail, the Irish transport companies. The Inter-Rail Card is valid 30 days in Europe for youths under 26 or senior citizens over 65—inquire at British Rail before your trip.

From North America

BY AIR: Travellers from almost every major American city and several Canadian cities can make connections to Dublin or Shannon through New York or Boston. Regular service is also available to Knock.

Charter Flights and Package Tours: Charter flights to Shannon, with connections to Dublin, feature even further air-fare reductions. FIT's (Foreign Independent Tours) offer low airfares and inexpensive travel within Ireland. Farmhouse tours are available with the traveller using vouchers to choose among over 200 farm and guest houses.

See TRAINS, p. 125, for information on Eurailpass and other unlimited-mileage rail tickets.

When to Go

The Gulf Stream is credited with keeping the Irish weather mild all year round, but accidents can happen. Readings as cold as −2 °F (−19 °C) and as hot as 92 °F (33 °C) have been recorded over the past century. May is usually the sunniest month, December the dullest. Tourists are in full flow in July and August; book well in advance for this period. At other times there's more scope for spontaneity.

Average monthly temperatures in Dublin:

	J	F	M	A	M	J	J	A	S	O	N	D
°F	41	41	43	47	51	56	59	58	56	50	45	43
°C	5	5	6	8	11	13	15	14	13	10	7	6

Planning Your Budget

To give you an idea of what to expect, here's a list of average prices in Irish pounds. They can only be approximate, however, as inflation creeps relentlessly up.

Accommodation. *Luxury hotel* (double with bath and breakfast) £60–100. *Medium hotel* (double with bath and breakfast) £35–55. *Guesthouses* (double with bath) £20–35. *Town and country homes, farmhouses, bed and breakfast* £9–15.

Airport transfer. Coach to Dublin £2.30, taxi to central Dublin £9.

Baby-sitter. £3 per hour.

Bicycle hire. £3 per day or £20 per week.

Buses. Local fares £1.80 (the most distant suburb). 8-day rail/bus rambler ticket for unlimited cross-country travel £52, 15-day ticket £77.

Camping. £5 per night.

Car hire (international company). *Fiat Uno* £35 per day, 24p per mile, £205 per week with unlimited mileage. *Opel Kadett* £44 per day, 26p per mile, £220 per week with unlimited mileage. Add 10% tax.

Cigarettes. £2 per packet of 20.

Entertainment. Cinema £2–3.50, discotheque, cabaret, nightclub £5, theatre ticket £5–10.

Ferry. Galway–Aran Islands £15, day return, £18 monthly return.

Hairdressers. *Woman's* wash and blow-dry £6, cut £10. *Man's* haircut, wash and dry £8.

Meals and drinks. Set-price lunch £5–10, dinner £8–15, carafe of wine £7, soft drink £1, pint of stout or beer £1.50, whiskey £1.10.

Museums, stately homes. £2.50 admission.

Shopping. Hand-knit wool sweater £50–65, hand-woven tweed £10–15 per yard.

Taxis. Minimum charge, Dublin £2. O'Connell Street to Heuston Station £4, Merrion Square to St. Patrick's Cathedral £4 (plus supplement for extra passengers, baggage, etc.).

Tours. Dublin city sightseeing, half-day, £10. Cork coach tour to Ring of Kerry £10.

Trains. Dublin–Cork £27.50, weekend return £23.50. 8-day rail rambler ticket for unlimited travel £52, 15-day ticket £77.

An A–Z Summary of Practical Information and Facts

> A star (*) following an entry indicates that relevant prices are to be found on page 105.

A

AIRPORTS*. International flights arrive at five airports of Ireland, in the east, south, west and north: Dublin, Cork, Shannon, Knock and Belfast.

Dublin Airport, about 7 miles north of the capital, is the busiest. Coaches link the airport with Busaras, the city bus terminal, every 20 minutes. The trip takes about half an hour. Taxi time between the airport and central Dublin is also about half an hour.

Dublin Airport has all the amenities that international travellers look for, starting with porters and push-it-yourself trolleys. Rounding out the facilities are a bank, car-hire desks, a church, hairdressers, nursery, post office, tourist information office, hotel-reservation desk, bars, restaurants and shops, including a duty-free shop and duty-free facilities for incoming passengers.

Shannon Airport, one of the first Atlantic gateways, lies about 15 miles west of Limerick. All the normal facilities are offered, as well as an unusually vast and varied duty-free shopping area.

Belfast Airport (Aldergrove) is 15 miles west of the city centre. Coach service into town every 80 minutes.

B

BICYCLE HIRE*. A network of dealers in all areas of the island encourages bike rental as a way of seeing "the real Ireland". Available are standard children's and adults' models, racing bikes and even tandems. Tourist information offices have a leaflet listing the participating dealers in more than 100 towns from Antrim to Cork. Motorbikes and mopeds cannot be hired in Ireland.

BOATS and FERRIES*. With over 3,000 miles of coastline and 9,000 miles of rivers and streams, Ireland is a boater's paradise. You might hire a fishing boat to take advantage of the excellent fresh-water and sea fishing. Or enjoy the country's scenic splendours in a rented cruiser (normally available with 2 to 8 berths). No boating permit is required for travel on the Shannon, and all companies offer a free piloting lesson. Points of departure include Carrick-on-Shannon, Athlone, Banagher and Killaloe.

The rugged islands off the coast of Ireland are rich in folklore, antiquities and natural wonders (especially birdlife). The Irish Tourist Board issues an information sheet, ''Island Boat Services'', listing numerous possibilities, including scheduled ferries. The Aran Islands are only a 30-mile steamer ride from Galway; crossings can also be made from Rossaveal, May to September. And there are connections by air as well (20 minutes). Garinish Island, noted for its exuberant vegetation, is 10 minutes away from Glengarriff (Co. Cork). Bad weather may interrupt ferry services.

BUSES*. The state-run Bus Eireann operates an extensive network of local, provincial and express bus routes, including cross-border services in conjunction with Northern Ireland's Ulsterbus Ltd. Service to destinations of touristic interest is increased in the summer. You can buy a pocket-sized timetable at bus stations and tourist information offices. Bus Atha Cliath/Dublin Bus runs Dublin Area Services. A separate book lists all bus and train routes in the Dublin district.

The bus services in Ireland cover almost every town and village. "Expressway" buses provide non-stop inter-city service, while "Provincial" vehicles make frequent stops in rural areas.

Iarnród Eireann-Irish Rail and Bus Eireann sell a **rambler** ticket, valid for either 8 or 15 days of unlimited cross-country bus and rail travel, and an **overlander** ticket with 15 days of unlimited travel in the Republic and also with Ulsterbus and Northern Ireland Railways (see also TRAINS).

On some buses in the Republic the destination is indicated in Irish only, so if you don't want to arrive in Gaillimh (Galway) instead of Gleann Garbh (Glengarriff), you'd better learn the correct Gaelic name before you start out. The timetable book has a useful glossary. On city buses, *An Lar* means "town centre".

The busiest bus routes in the cities use double-deckers, on which you take a seat and wait for the conductor to come and collect the proper fare. On single-deckers you pay the driver as you enter.

As in Britain, queues are taken seriously. Ireland's official Queueing Regulations of 1961 rule that six or more persons waiting for a bus must queue two abreast in an orderly manner. The queue faces the direction from which the bus will arrive, except where the bus stop sign indicates otherwise.

C **CAMPING and CARAVANNING*.** Officially approved camping sites in Ireland range from fairly spartan layouts to resort-style parks with tennis courts, mini-golf, shops and nearby beaches. If the "no vacancy" sign is posted, take heart: many a farmer will let campers spend the night on his property, but always ask permission. At some camp sites, and at rental agencies, touring caravans (trailers) may be hired by the day or week. If you're pulling your own, note that the connections for Calor gas tanks are not suitable for the cylinders sold in Ireland. Lists of camping and caravanning parks and their facilities are available from tourist information offices or:

Irish Caravan Council, 2 Offington Court, Sutton, Dublin 13, tel. (01) 323776
Northern Ireland Tourist Board, 48 High Street, Belfast BT1 2DS, tel. (0232) 231221

Horse-drawn caravans, in which tourists can live and travel like gypsies, may be hired by the week. They are most commonly found in the west and south-west of Ireland. Bookings should be made in advance through:

Central Reservation Service, Irish Tourist Board, Baggot Street Bridge, Dublin 2, tel. (01) 76 58 71

CAR HIRE*. Dozens of car hire companies operate at airports and in the towns, dealing in everything from minicars to so-called executive cars and vans. The internationally known firms usually have slightly higher rates than their local competitors. Some companies permit cars to be picked up in one place and handed in elsewhere.

Most companies have a two-tiered tariff, raising prices by as much as 10% to 20% for the "high season" in summer. In any season, cars may be hired on a "time-plus-mileage" basis or with unlimited mileage. If you're unsure whether you'll be chalking up enough travelling to justify the "unlimited" rate, the firm may agree to let you choose the more favourable tariff retroactively.

A valid national licence, normally at least two years old, is required. Many firms permit 21-year-old drivers to hire cars, but the minimum age can be as high as 25. The maximum age, depending on the company, ranges from 65 to 70. Credit cards are usually accepted in lieu of a deposit.

Rental rates include third-party liability insurance. Additional coverage can be arranged on the spot. Comprehensive cover is recommended.

108   Don't forget: Drive on the left and use your seat belts.

CIGARETTES, CIGARS, TOBACCO★. Irish, British and foreign brands of cigarettes are widely available, as are imported cigars and pipe tobacco. They are highly taxed, so smokers who pass a duty-free shop on the way to Ireland should stock up in advance. Local brands include *Sweet Afton* (unfiltered), *Carroll's No. 1* (filtered) and *Benson & Hedges Extra Length* (luxury filter).

Smoking is restricted in many public places. Some railway carriages and all buses are marked as non-smoking areas.

CLOTHING★. Matching the easy-going way of life, habits of dress are relatively casual in Ireland. Women may want to wear a long skirt in the evening but otherwise the accent is on comfort in both clothes and shoes. Avant-garde fashions are slow to arrive in Ireland. Men are advised to wear a suit or jacket with tie for an evening out but nothing more formal than a sweater or sports jacket in the daytime. A raincoat or umbrella will come in handy. Also keep in mind that the evenings, even in midsummer, can be quite nippy, so sweaters and coats are in order. If you haven't brought along enough warm clothing, you can always pick up a handsome homespun tweed or rugged Aran sweater.

Ireland is in transition to the metric system, so most clothes are marked in both old Imperial (British) and new European measurements. Following is a comparison of Irish/British and American sizes. Remember however that sizes may vary according to manufacturers. Men's suit and shirt sizes are the same in the U.S. and Ireland.

Women's clothes					
Eire/U.K.	10/32	12/34	14/36	16/38	18/40
U.S.A.	8/32	10/34	12/36	14/38	16/40
Women's footwear					
Eire/U.K.	3	4	5	6	7
U.S.A.	$4^1/_2$	$5^1/_2$	$6^1/_2$	$7^1/_2$	$8^1/_2$
Men's footwear					
Eire/U.K.	6	7	8	9	10
U.S.A.	$6^1/_2$	$7^1/_2$	$8^1/_2$	$9^1/_2$	$10^1/_2$

COMMUNICATIONS

Post Office. An Post operates all post office services in the Republic. Most postboxes are pillar-shaped (a few antiques still have Queen Victoria's monogram on them), and painted green. Most post offices are open from 9 a.m. to 5.30 p.m. but the main office—the historic

C General Post Office in O'Connell Street, Dublin—is open until 8 p.m. six days a week (6.30 p.m. on Sundays). Postcard shops and news-agents sometimes sell stamps, too. In some areas a post office may be identified by a sign in Irish only—*Oifig an Phoist*.

If you don't know where you'll be staying, you can have mail sent to you "poste restante" (general delivery) to any town. Letters sent "poste restante" to the G.P.O. in Dublin may be collected up to 8 p.m.

In Northern Ireland the postboxes are red. Note that Eire stamps may not be used on mail posted in Northern Ireland and British stamps are invalid in the Republic.

Telegrams. The traditional telegram has been replaced by the tele-message. Dial 196 and it will be delivered with the next day's post. The telemessage is accepted at post offices, with similar speed of delivery.

Telephone. Public telephones are found in post offices, hotels, stores and on the street. In the Republic the sentry-box booths, cream-coloured with green trim, as well as the more modern aluminium and glass booths now increasingly used, are marked in Gaelic, TELEFON.

Instructions for operating coin telephones are usually given. For payphones now in use throughout Ireland, use 10p or 50p coins for direct dialling of local, national and international calls. Operator assistance is available by dialling 10.

In Northern Ireland public telephones are found in metal and glass booths or yellow cubicles. Old-style red kiosks are increasingly rare. They operate with 5p, 10p, 50p coins and phonecards. Do not deposit money until the connection has been made; a series of rapid pips will indicate when the machine is ready to accept your coins.

COMPLAINTS. Your first move, of course, would be to complain to the manager of the offending establishment. But if this fails to give satisfaction, turn to your nearest tourist office. Complaints in writing may be directed to:

Customer Relations Section, Irish Tourist Board, Baggot Street Bridge, Dublin 2

Northern Ireland Tourist Board, River House, 48 High Street, Belfast BT1 2DS

CONVERTER CHARTS. The metric system is being introduced in Ireland but with some resistance from traditionalists. Beer and milk may be ordered by the litre or by the pint (0.568 litre) and petrol (gasoline) by the litre. Other commodities have gone over entirely to metric measures. Temperatures are measured exclusively in Celsius. For fluid measures, see page 113.

Temperature

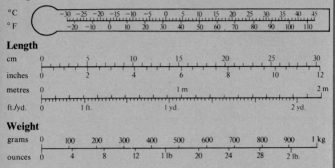

°C

°F

Length

cm

inches

metres

ft./yd.

Weight

grams

ounces

CRIME and THEFT. The Crime Prevention Office of the Garda Siochana (police) warns visitors to carry only minimum amounts of cash and jewellery. Pickpockets operate in crowded stores and markets, at bus stops and sports events. The Gardai say tourists who leave property unattended in cars risk losses; they suggest parking in well-lit and busy areas and keeping valuables out of sight. Thefts from hotel rooms are rare.

CUSTOMS and ENTRY FORMALITIES. Citizens of many countries, from Andorra to Zambia, are admitted to the Irish Republic without visas. Formalities on arrival are minimal. British travellers arriving in the Republic directly from Britain require no passport or identity card, but others should have valid documents. If you arrive from an infected area of the world, you will need proof of vaccination. It is forbidden to import pornographic material or books listed by the Eire government's censor (the list is now much shorter than in years past). You may bring as much Irish currency as you wish into the country, but may only take out up to 100 Irish pounds. The amount of foreign currency brought in can be taken out, plus the equivalent of 500 Irish pounds (traveller's cheques excluded). These conditions do

C not apply to passengers travelling between Ireland and Great Britain, the Channel Islands or the Isle of Man.·

The following chart indicates what you may take into Eire duty-free, and, when returning home, into your own country:

Into:	Cigarettes		Cigars		Tobacco	Spirits	Wine
Eire 1)	300	or	75	or	400 g.	1.5 l. and 5 l.	
2)	200	or	50	or	250 g.	1 l. and 2 l.	
3)	400	or	100	or	500 g.	1 l. and 2 l.	
Australia	200	or	250 g.or		250 g.	1 l. or 1 l.	
Canada	200	and	50	and	900 g.	1.1 l. or 1.1 l.	
N. Zealand	200	or	50	or	250 g.	1.1 l. and 4.5 l.	
S. Africa	400	and	50	and	250 g.	1 l. and 2 l.	
U.K.	200	or	50	or	250 g.	1 l. and 2 l.	
U.S.A.	200	and	100	and	4)	1 l. or 1 l.	

1) residents of European countries with goods bought inside EEC not tax free
2) residents of European countries with goods bought tax free
3) residents of countries outside Europe
4) a reasonable quantity

The customs restrictions between Eire and Northern Ireland are normally limited to animals and agricultural products. Motorists are likely to undergo security checks at any of the 20 approved border crossings between the Republic and Northern Ireland and are warned to avoid unauthorized crossing points.

D **DRIVING IN IRELAND.** Traffic moves on the left, though not all Irish drivers worry about this formality. Thousands of motorists in the Republic received their licences without ever having taken a test, and it shows in their sometimes frightening driving habits. In fairness, though, competent foreign drivers perplexed by country roadsigns (occasionally in Gaelic only) can also be a hazard.

Importing your car. Be sure to have the registration papers and insurance coverage. The usual formula is the Green Card, an extension to the normal insurance making it valid in other countries. Your car should also have a nationality plate on the back. Virtually any valid driving licence from any country is recognized in Ireland.

Driving conditions. If you're not accustomed to driving on the left, be extra careful for the first few days, especially when turning corners and at roundabouts (traffic circles).

Driving on country roads can be an extremely pleasurable experience, but always keep alert for the unexpected: cattle camped in the roadway, tractors inching along or ambling pedestrians.

On zebra crossings (marked by amber beacons), pedestrians have the right of way.

Beware of bicycles weaving in and out of town traffic; cyclists make their own rules here.

Speed limits. Unless otherwise marked, the limit in the Irish Republic is 55 mph (88 kph) on the open road and 30 or 40 mph (48 or 64 kph) in towns and built-up areas. The same town limits apply in Northern Ireland, where the limit for roads in the country is 60 mph (96 kph). On dual carriageways and motorways, the limit is 70 mph (112 kph).

Parking. Ever more of a problem, especially in Dublin and other big cities. Parking meters in Dublin have instructions printed on them. Some other towns have zones requiring "discs" or variations on this time-limit system. Check the signs giving regulations.

If you leave your car on a yellow line during business hours you may be fined for parking in a no-parking zone. If you leave your car on a double line, meaning "no waiting", it may be towed away; you will have to pay a fine plus towing charges. Be especially careful of the regulations in Northern Ireland, where some areas are off-limits to cars. And you should know that Northern Ireland's "no unattended vehicles" warnings really mean business. The security forces don't tow away suspicious cars, they detonate them.

Fuel. In some areas finding a filling station open on a Sunday may be a problem, so best top up on Saturday for weekend excursions. Petrol (gasoline) is sold by the litre.

Fluid measures

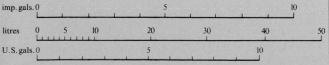

D **Distances.** Here are approximate road distances in miles/kilometres between Dublin and other important centres; plus approximate hours of driving time:

Dublin–Belfast	104/167	3 hr.
Dublin–Cork	160/257	4¹/₂ hr.
Dublin–Galway	136/219	4 hr.
Dublin–Rosslare Harbour	101/163	3 hr.

Seat belts. Drivers and front-seat passengers must wear seat belts in the Republic; non-use may be punished by a fine.

Drinking and driving. Police on both sides of the border are strict about this. Any driver suspected of being affected by drink is subjected to a roadside "breathalyser" test. Those who fail—and it only takes a pint or two of beer—risk heavy fines or jail or both. The crackdown affects visitors as well as residents.

Road signs. Many of the international picture-signs are in use on Irish highways. Road direction signs in the Republic are almost always bilingual, English and Gaelic, but in some Irish-speaking enclaves the English may be omitted. Traditional road signs give distances in miles but the new white-on-green signs are in kilometres (with a small "km" to remind you).

Some written signs may not be instantly comprehensible to transatlantic or European visitors:

Ireland	*U.S.A.*
Clearway	No parking along highway
Cul de sac	Dead end
Dual carriageway	Divided highway
Layby	Rest area
Level crossing	Rail crossing
Loose chippings	Loose gravel
No overtaking	No passing
Road up	Under construction
Roadworks	Men working
Soft edges (or **margin**)	Soft shoulder

E **ELECTRIC CURRENT.** Standard current everywhere is 220-volt, 50-cycle. Hotels usually have special sockets for shavers, running at both 220 and 110 volts. Certain appliances may need a converter. Adaptor plugs may be required to fit Ireland's two types of wall outlets—3-pin flat and 2-pin round.

114

EMBASSIES and CONSULATES. The Dublin telephone directory lists foreign embassies and consular services under the heading "Diplomatic and Consular Missions". Consular agencies in provincial towns are all listed in Part 2 of the directory under the same heading.

Principal embassies and consulates in Dublin:

Australia: Fitzwilton House, Wilton Terrace, Dublin 2, tel. (01) 761517
Canada: 65/68 St. Stephen's Green, Dublin 2, tel. (01) 781988
Great Britain: 33 Merrion Road, Dublin 4, tel. (01) 695211
U.S.A.: 42 Elgin Road, Dublin 4, tel. (01) 688777

Consulates in Northern Ireland:

U.S.A.: Queen's House, Queen Street, Belfast 1, tel. (0232) 328239

EMERGENCIES. For police, fire brigade or ambulance, dial 999 from any telephone in Ireland (no coin required). Tell the emergency operator which service you need. See also individual entries such as EMBASSIES and CONSULATES, HEALTH and MEDICAL CARE, etc.

GUIDES. Organized guided tours are conducted at some major attractions as part of the admission fee. A great variety of excursions, led by competent guides, cover all the major monuments and beauty spots by coach. Tourist offices have schedules. The tourist office in Dublin can also give you a list of qualified guides.

HAIRDRESSERS and BARBERS*. The trend toward combined men's and women's hairdressing salons has not bypassed Ireland. But there are still many segregated holdouts, including old-fashioned, no-frill barber shops for men only, announced by a rotating red-and-white-striped barber pole. Prices are often higher in the big towns.

HEALTH and MEDICAL CARE. Residents of EEC countries are covered by reciprocal health care in Ireland. Visitors from mainland Europe should bring a completed E111 form. No form is required for U.K. visitors. Others should have some form of hospital insurance. Many package tours provide inexpensive temporary policies.

Hotels usually know which local doctors are available. But in an emergency you can always dial 999 to find a doctor on call. In Dublin at least one hospital is always open for emergency cases; again, the operator at 999 can tell you which hospital is "on duty".

H The Dublin Dental Hospital, Lincoln Place, Dublin 2, tel. (01) 682211, takes dental emergency cases from 9 to 11 a.m. and 2 to 4 p.m.

Chemists' (pharmacies) normally operate during shopping hours only. But a few stay open until 10 p.m., and some are open from 11 a.m. to 1 p.m. or 10 p.m. on Sundays. Details of rota arrangements are given in chemists' windows.

HITCH-HIKING. Chances are reasonably good that a hitch-hiker will get a lift in Ireland, but the practice is discouraged. There is no law against it except on the motorways (expressways) of Northern Ireland.

HOTELS and ACCOMMODATION★. Exploring Ireland you can stay in a super-luxury hotel one night, a family-run guest house the next and a thatched cottage after that. Efficient tourist offices will handle spur-of-the-moment or long-range reservations for you. The tourist boards inspect and classify all hostelries and issue brochures, free or at minimal cost, listing all the approved establishments with information about their rates and facilities. Tariffs are government-controlled, and the maximum rate shown in the brochure is the highest which proprietors may charge.

Hotel bills usually include a service charge. Value Added Tax on the total cost of accommodation, meals and service is included in the tariffs.

Hotels and motor hotels. These are officially graded in five categories:

A★: most luxurious with high standard of cuisine and services

A: extremely comfortable with experienced service

B★: well-furnished, good service, private bath available but not necessarily in the majority of rooms

B: well-kept, limited but good cuisine and service

C: clean and comfortable, hot and cold running water

Hotels and motels too new to have been classified are listed ungraded.

Guest houses. Usually family-run with friendly personal service, can include full board for resident guests. These establishments are also listed and graded.

Irish Homes. The Irish Tourist Board issues *Guest Accommodation,* a 114-page book covering hotels, guest houses, youth hostels, town and country homes and farmhouses. The Northern Ireland Tourist

Board publishes two similar brochures, *All the places to stay* and *Farm and Country House Holidays.* As to Bed and Breakfast, you don't need any brochures to find them—you'll see signs all over the place.

Thatched cottages. This scheme operates mainly in the west of Ireland near beauty spots in five counties. Details available from tourist offices or:

Rent-an-Irish Cottage Ltd., Shannon Free Airport, Co. Clare, tel. (061) 61588

Youth hostels. The Irish Youth Hostels Association runs about 50 hostels in the Republic. Membership cards issued by national youth hostel associations overseas are required. An official handbook is available from the association's head office:

39 Mountjoy Square, Dublin 1

There are a dozen youth hostels in Northern Ireland. Details from:
Youth Hostel Information, 56 Bradbury Place, Belfast BT7 1RV

HOURS. The hours of operation of shops and offices vary with the season and the location.

Shops in the cities are normally open from 9 a.m. to 5.30 p.m., Monday to Saturday; country towns have one early closing day. The big shopping centres often stay open until 9 p.m. Thursday and Friday. Smaller shops, particularly groceries and newsagents, often open on Sundays, many until 1 p.m.

Offices and businesses operate from 9 a.m. to 5.30 p.m., Monday to Friday (and on Saturdays as well in some cases). Tourist information offices are open from 10 a.m. to 6 p.m. with longer summer hours in the busiest places.

Banks. In general banks are open Monday to Friday, 10 a.m. to 12.30 p.m. and 1.30 to 3 p.m. Most towns have late opening day once a week (Thursday in Dublin) when the banks stay open until 5 p.m. Some banks remain open over the lunch hour. In Northern Ireland the banks are open from 10 a.m. to 3.30 p.m. Outside Belfast, branches may close for lunch. The bank at Dublin Airport is open every day of the year except Christmas, from 6.45 a.m. to 10.30 p.m.

Pubs. Licensing hours have been streamlined. In the Republic, winter hours are 10.30 a.m.–11 p.m., with an extra half hour in summer.

H On Sundays all year, pubs are open from 12.30 p.m. to 2 p.m. and from 4 p.m. to 11 p.m. In addition, there is half-an-hour drinking-up time in the evenings, all year round. In Northern Ireland, pubs are open Monday to Saturday 11 a.m.–11 p.m., all year. Sunday opening, a new departure, is from 12.30 p.m. to 2.30 p.m., and from 7.30 p.m. to 10 p.m., all year. In addition, there is half-an-hour drinking-up time.

Museums, stately homes, sites. Museums and stately homes follow no general rule except that visiting hours are often curtailed in winter. There are no universal days when these institutions are closed, though Sunday, Monday or Tuesday are the most probable. To avoid disappointment always check first with the nearest tourist information office.

L **LANGUAGE.** English is spoken with lilting Irish accents everywhere in Ireland. In the Gaeltacht areas of the west and south, the principal language is Irish, though almost everyone there is also fluent in English. Bilingualism is officially encouraged in the Republic. Summer courses in the Irish language are given in the Gaeltacht. For information, write:

Comhdhail Naisiunta na Gaeilge, 86 Sraid Gardner Iocht, Baile Atha Cliath 1, Eire

Postmen are bilingual, too; Baile Atha Cliath is the Irish name for the city of Dublin.

Here is a short Irish glossary to help you read the signs:

Irish/Gaelic	English
ar(d)	high place
ath	ford of river
baile, bally	hamlet, group of houses, town
beann, ben	mountain peak
cairn	mound of stones atop prehistoric tomb
carrick, carrig	rock
cather	fort
clachan, clochan	small group of dwellings; stepping stones across a river; beehive-shaped hut
clon, cluain	meadow
corrach	marsh or low plain
corrie	circular hollow with steep sides

currach	small boat
derry, dare	oak tree or wood
donagh	church
drum, drom	ridge, hillock
dun, doon	fort
ennis, inch, innis(h)	island
keel, kill, caol	narrow
kil, kill, cill	church; monk's cell
lough	lake, sea inlet
mol, mull	height
ros	promontory or wood
sceillig, skellig	crag, rock
sliabh, slieve	mountain
tulach, tully	hillock

LAUNDRY and DRY-CLEANING. Hotels in Ireland provide the usual laundry and cleaning services. As elsewhere, they often charge extra for "express" service. Commercial laundries, dry-cleaning establishments and self-service launderettes can be found in most towns. If you're too busy to hang around a launderette you can usually arrange a "service wash" for a small extra charge, permitting you to return in a couple of hours and pick up your washed, dried and sometimes folded clothes.

LOST PROPERTY. The place to go in search of any lost property is normally the local police station. But public transport organizations sometimes have their own lost property departments. For items left on trains and buses based in Dublin, try:
Lost property office, 98 Marlboro Street, Dublin 1, tel. (01) 720000

The main lost property office in Belfast is at Musgrave Street R.V.C. (police) station, tel. (0232) 237212.

MAPS. Tourist offices sell maps of Ireland for very little; car hire firms often give them to their clients. Extremely detailed regional maps on a scale of 1:250,000 are also sold at tourist offices and many bookshops and news-agents. Hotels and local tourist information offices often issue free maps of the towns and nearby attractions.

Street signs in Dublin are written in both English and Irish. A consecutive numbering system is still in use on houses in some of the older streets, going up one side of the street and down the other.

The maps in this book were specially created by Falk-Verlag.

M **MEETING PEOPLE.** The Irish have time enough for conversation and a touch of the blarney, so getting to know them should be no problem. An easy and pleasant way to absorb the feeling of the country is to stay at farmhouses or town and country homes approved and listed by the tourist authorities. If you are interested in specialized aspects of Irish life, you can arrange this by writing in advance to:

Irish Tourist Board, Baggot Street Bridge, Dublin 2

Boy-meets-girl opportunities occur at the usual places—pubs, cabarets, dances. However, traditions of conservative behaviour are maintained more strictly than in some other European societies.

MONEY MATTERS

Currency. The symbol for the Irish pound (or *punt*) of the Republic is abbreviated £; in Northern Ireland the British pound sterling (£) is used. Both are divided into 100 pence (p). British and Irish coins are identically sized and shaped and sometimes slip across the border, but the currencies are no longer interchangeable. Banks everywhere on the island are accustomed to exchanging *punts* and pounds.

Irish banknotes are issued in 1, 5, 10, 20, 50 and 100 pound denominations. Coins come in 1p, 2p, 5p, 10p, 20p and the heptagonal 50p piece.

Banks and currency exchange. All major banks provide exchange facilities. Major post offices, including the GPO in Dublin, have a *Bureau de change.* Some international travel agencies also change money and traveller's cheques. Be sure to take along your passport as proof of identity when cashing traveller's cheques. See also HOURS.

The O'Connell Street Tourist Information Office in Dublin and the Cork Office in Grand Parade also operate money exchange services. The Dublin office will change your money from 9 a.m. to 5.15 p.m., Monday to Friday. The Cork office provides this facility from 9 a.m. to 1.15 p.m. and 2.30 p.m. to 5.15 p.m., Monday to Friday.

Credit cards and traveller's cheques are widely accepted in Irish shops, hotels, restaurants and car-hire firms. **Eurocheques** are accepted in many hotels and stores and in all banks.

Tipping. Most hotels and restaurants include service charge, which makes tipping unnecessary, though good service may merit an additional gratuity. It's appropriate to tip bellboys, filling-station attendants, etc., for extra services.

Some further indications:

Hairdresser/Barber	10%
Lavatory attendant	20p
Maid, per week	£2 for extra services
Porter, per bag	50p
Taxi driver	10%
Tour guide	10–15%

NEWSPAPERS and MAGAZINES. Three national morning papers are published in Dublin—the *Irish Independent*, the *Irish Press* and the comprehensive *Irish Times*. The *Cork Examiner* is also considered a national daily. Northern Ireland has two morning dailies, the *News Letter* and the *Irish News*. Local entertainment news is well covered in the *Evening Herald* and *Evening Press* of Dublin, the *Evening Echo* of Cork and the *Belfast Telegraph*. Dublin and Belfast Sunday papers are also useful.

Visitors to Dublin may also find detailed topical information about what's on in the fortnightly magazine *In Dublin*.

Britain's national daily and Sunday newspapers are sold almost everywhere in Ireland on the morning of publication. Leading newsagents in the major towns also sell a range of European newspapers and magazines as well as European and American magazines.

PETS. Unless you and Fido are resident in Britain, forget about taking your pet with you on holiday to Ireland. As a precaution against rabies, Ireland bars the entry of all dogs and cats except those coming from Britain (which has similar severe quarantine laws). Other visiting animals must undergo six months of isolation before they are allowed to mingle with the rabies-free Irish dogs and cats.

PHOTOGRAPHY. All those green fields, blue skies and white clouds make beautiful pictures. If you run out of film you'll find all the well-known brands on sale.

Be sure to ask permission before you take photos in museums and historic churches; sometimes flashbulbs are forbidden. Military bases are off-limits to photographers. In Northern Ireland you should avoid pointing your camera, or anything else, at personnel or installations of the security forces.

P **POLICE.** The official name of the civic guard, or police force, of the Irish Republic is the Garda Siochana, less formally known as the Garda (pronounced "gorda"). Except for extraordinary assignments they are unarmed. There is no special police unit detailed to help tourists.

In Northern Ireland the police force is the Royal Ulster Constabulary (R.U.C.).

In case of emergency, telephone 999, in both the Republic and Northern Ireland.

PUBLIC HOLIDAYS

For both **Eire** and **Northern Ireland**:		
Jan. 1	New Year's Day	*Movable:*
Mar. 17	St. Patrick's Day	Good Friday
Dec. 25	Christmas Day	Easter Monday
Dec. 26	Boxing Day	

Eire only:

June Bank Holiday (first Monday of June), August Bank Holiday (first Monday of August), October Bank Holiday (last Monday in October).

Northern Ireland only:

May Day (first Monday of May), Spring Bank Holiday (last Monday of May), Orangemen's Day (July 12), Summer Bank Holiday (last Monday of August).

R **RADIO and TV.** Radio Telefis Eireann (RTE), a state-run organization, is the largest broadcaster in the Republic, though cable television has greatly expanded viewing possibilities. Most programmes are in English except for a few Irish or bilingual Irish-English broadcasts. Foreign films are sometimes shown in the original language with English subtitles. In Northern Ireland the BBC and rival commercial stations are on the air.

RTE operates three radio stations primarily in English as well as Radio na Gaeltachta with an all-Irish programme. The BBC runs five radio stations in Northern Ireland. There are also commercial channels aimed at audiences north and south of the border.

Transistors and car radios can pick up the principal radio stations of Europe; reception is best at night.

RELIGIOUS SERVICES. About 95% of the people in the Irish Republic are Catholic. Of these a big percentage not only go to mass every Sunday but drop into church informally during weekdays. Sunday Mass can be heard somewhere in Dublin almost any time of the day or night, from 6 a.m. to 9 p.m., in English, and sometimes Irish.

Dublin's two cathedrals belong to the Church of Ireland, which is Anglican. Schedules of services at these and other Protestant churches are available in all hotels, with further details in the Saturday newspapers. Dublin has churches of more than a dozen Protestant sects as well as a Greek Orthodox church, synagogues and an Islamic centre.

In Northern Ireland, Catholics comprise slightly less than one-third of the population. But they outnumber the largest single Protestant group, the Presbyterians, as well as the Church of Ireland.

Both the Catholic church and the Church of Ireland are organized on an island-wide basis, ignoring the frontier. The ecclesiastic capital of Ireland is Armagh, in the North, which has two cathedrals, one Catholic and the other Church of Ireland. Both are called St. Patrick's.

TAXIS*. Irish taxis may be found cruising the streets, but the majority park at designated taxi ranks waiting for clients to come to them; taxis can also be contacted by telephone (see classified telephone directory under "Taxicabs—Ranks and Shelters"). Many towns also have radio-dispatched taxis, but these charge extra for the mileage on the way to pick up the client. Fares vary from town to town. Dublin and Cork have metered taxis while smaller towns have standard fares or charges by agreement. A very few Dublin taxi drivers have been known to add imaginary supplements to the fare. You should pay only the charge on the meter, plus if applicable, supplements for extra passengers, additional luggage, waiting time, and trips on public holidays or after midnight.

Radio-cab dispatchers in Dublin can be reached at: 761111, 683333, 766666 or 783333.

TIME DIFFERENCES. As a daylight-saving measure, Ireland sets its clocks one hour ahead from mid-March to the end of October. The rest of the year the country is on GMT (Greenwich Mean Time).

Summer time differences				
New York	**Dublin**	Jo'burg	Sydney	Auckland
7 a.m.	**noon**	1 p.m.	9 p.m.	11 p.m.

T **TOILETS.** Public conveniences are relatively abundant in the towns of Ireland. Look for the direction sign, "Public Toilets". The only hitch is that the gender signs on doors in the Republic may be printed in Gaelic, not English. *Mna* should not be misconstrued as a misprint for "men"; it's Gaelic for "ladies". *Fir* means "gentlemen".

TOURIST INFORMATION. Tourist information offices all over Ireland are ready to provide travel information and advice, booklets, maps and a hotel reservation service (for a small charge) extending to horse-drawn caravans and self-drive cabin cruisers. They are usually open from 10 a.m. to 6 p.m. though many local offices operate only in the summer. For general inquiries, write:

Irish Tourist Board—Bord Failte
P. O. Box 273
Dublin 8
or
Northern Ireland Tourist Board
48 High Street
Belfast BT1 2DS

Following are the addresses of tourist information offices in Ireland and abroad.

Irish Tourist Board Offices

Canada: 10 King Street East, Toronto M5C 1C3, tel. (416) 364-1301

United Kingdom: 150 New Bond Street, London W1Y OAQ, tel. (01) 493-3201 and (01) 629-7292

U.S.A.: 757 Third Avenue, New York, NY 10017, tel. (212) 418-0800

Australia: MLC Centre, 38th Level, Martin Place, Sydney 2000, tel. (02) 232-7177

New Zealand: P.O. Box 279, Auckland 1, tel. (09) 793-708

Regional headquarters, Ireland

Dublin and Eastern: 14 Upper O'Connell Street, Dublin, tel. (01) 747733
1 Clarinda Park North, Dun Laoghaire, tel. (01) 808571

South-eastern: 41 The Quay, Waterford, tel. (051) 75823

Cork/Kerry: Tourist House, Grand Parade, Cork, tel. (021) 273251

Mid-western: Granary Centre, Michael Street, Limerick, tel. (061) 317522

Western: Aras Failte, Eyre Square, Galway, tel. (091) 63081
Sligo: Aras Reddan, Temple Street, Sligo, tel. (071) 61201
Midland: Dublin Road, Mullingar, tel. (062) 48761

The Irish Tourist Board has two offices in Northern Ireland, at 53 Castle Street, Belfast BT1 1GH, tel. (0232) 327888 and 40 Foyle Street, Londonderry BT48 6AR, tel. (0504) 369501.

For **Northern Ireland** tourist information:

Northern Ireland Tourist Board, River House, 48 High Street, Belfast BT1 2DS, tel. (0232) 231221

11 Berkeley Street, London W1X 6BU, tel. 493-0601

You may also address your inquiries to offices of the British Tourist Authority the world over.

TRAINS*. Passenger lines in Ireland have been cut back to the main routes, but cross-country service to and from Dublin can be quick and comfortable. The main inter-city routes have air-conditioned, sound-proofed expresses. There are two classes on through-trains: Standard (2nd class) and Super Standard (1st class). Iarnród Eireann-Irish Rail, the Irish railway company, sells 8-day and 15-day **rambler** tickets, good for unlimited rail travel, or rail and bus travel at a higher price. A book of train timetables is on sale at railway stations and tourist offices.

    Note: Dublin has two main-line railway stations (Heuston Station and Connolly Station) as well as commuter-line stations, so be sure to check in advance for the correct terminal.

Some trip times on express trains:

Dublin–Belfast:	2 hr. 10 min.
Dublin–Cork:	2 hr. 30 min.
Dublin–Galway:	2 hr. 50 min.
Dublin–Waterford:	2 hr. 35 min.

Ireland has now joined the group of countries honouring the **Eurail-pass,** a flat-rate unlimited mileage ticket, valid for first-class rail travel anywhere in Western Europe outside the U.K. **Eurail Youthpass** is similar to the Eurailpass, but offers second-class travel at a cheaper rate to anyone under 26. This ticket is available to visitors from outside Europe.

Index

An asterisk (*) next to a page number indicates a map reference. For index to Practical Information, see inside front cover.

INDEX